THE
STERLING
REDEMPTION

By the same author

The Sterling Years: Small Arms and the Men
1992, Leo Cooper
Reprinted 2011, Pen & Sword Military

THE STERLING REDEMPTION

Twenty-Five Years to Clear My Name

James Edmiston
and Lawrence Kormornick

Pen & Sword
MILITARY

First published in Great Britain in 2012 by
PEN & SWORD MILITARY
an imprint of
Pen & Sword Books Ltd
47 Church Street
Barnsley
South Yorkshire
S70 2AS

Website: www.thesterlingredemption.com

ISBN 978 1 78159 027 0

Typeset in Ehrhardt
by Chic Media Ltd

Printed and bound in England
by the MPG Books Group

Pen & Sword Books Ltd incorporates the imprints of
Pen & Sword Aviation, Pen & Sword Family History, Pen & Sword Maritime,
Pen & Sword Military, Pen & Sword Discovery, Wharncliffe Local History,
Wharncliffe True Crime, Wharncliffe Transport, Pen & Sword Select,
Pen & Sword Military Classics, Leo Cooper, Remember When,
The Praetorian Press, Seaforth Publishing and Frontline Publishing

For a complete list of Pen & Sword titles please contact
PEN & SWORD BOOKS LIMITED
47 Church Street, Barnsley, South Yorkshire, S70 2AS England
E-mail: enquiries@pen-and-sword.co.uk
Website: www.pen-and-sword.co.uk

Contents

Acknowledgements

I would like to thank all those who helped James through his struggle to achieve justice. I would also like to thank Linne Matthews and Paul Rosenberg, who were wonderful editors.

My family, who lived through the case for more than ten years with someone who for so long was distracted and at times obsessed, also deserve thanks.

I dedicate my part in this book to them.

Lawrence Kormornick

Note on Sources

The Sterling Redemption is based upon transcripts of evidence given to and the findings of (i) the Scott Inquiry into the export of Defence Equipment and Dual-Use Goods to Iraq and Related Prosecutions and (ii) the Court of Appeal (Criminal) and upon documents filed with the Inquiry and the Court. It is also based on decisions of the Home Secretary and Independent Assessor.

Introduction

The Home Office,
London SW1, 25 August 2008

The autumn sun glinted through the open window of my green and black Mini Clubman as I sped south along the Mall past Buckingham Palace and across Victoria to collect a letter. The city flashed by as I tried to clear my thoughts. A relaxing Italian lunch at Zizzi in Wigmore Street had done little to ease my anxiety.

I, James Stuart Moray Edmiston, had waited twenty-five years for this moment and the letter would affect the rest of my life. In the passenger seat, my lawyer, Lawrence Kormornick, was also lost in deep reflection. Having laboured on the case for more than ten years, it had become a crusade for him. Would the outcome justify all the time and effort he had expended and bring closure to the interminable suffering of his client, he wondered. The Mini turned into Marsham Street and stopped suddenly outside the Home Office.

"You get it, Lawrence. I'll keep the traffic wardens at bay. Don't be long," I requested. Kormornick quickly disappeared into the nearby monolithic structure that personified the faceless mass of government.

He seemed to be taking ages. My thoughts began to drift back again in a haze over the events of the past twenty-five years. Life had been a living hell; a nightmare. Crisis had followed crisis, and what was in that letter would determine whether my remaining years would also be spent in penury. There had been absolutely no hint of what the letter would say.

Twenty-five years is a long sentence – two life sentences for murder, in fact. Can the loss of that length of time ever be quantified adequately? Though compensation was important to me, some form of apology was also expected.

Suddenly, Kormornick reappeared looking excited. "I've got it," he shouted, clutching an insignificant looking, common brown Civil Service envelope. "Here, it's yours. You open it."

I grabbed the envelope, pondered diffidently, and hesitated, fingering it gingerly.

"Get on with it, let's not wait another twenty-five years," Kormornick remonstrated ironically. Slowly, putting my finger into the envelope, I peeled the flap open. Taking out the letter and Final Assessment, beads of sweat were forming on my brow. The Assessor's summary concluded:

> The circumstances of this application reveal a miscarriage of justice that has led to a personal tragedy, a broken family and the loss of a business ... I am quite satisfied that there was misconduct in the investigation and prosecution of this case involving government officials ...

After twenty-five years, it was so important for me and my family to receive some official acknowledgment of the harm done to us by those government officials. I was completely lost in thought as I read the details of the award.

"Well…?" insisted Kormornick.

Chapter 1

The MOD Exhibition in Aqaba, Jordan, February 1983

"Where are the Sterlings, Mr Edmiston?" asked the general, firmly but politely.

I, James Edmiston, the 39-year-old managing director of the Sterling Armament Company, was standing at my company's exhibition booth aboard a "floater" – a floating exhibition on a ro-ro ship chartered from Townsend Thoresen by the Ministry of Defence. British defence equipment was on display and being toured around to friendly countries in the Middle East. This was my first trip to Jordan and meeting Jordanian Army officers again could produce some more orders.

General Hilmi Lozi and Colonel Fawzi Baj had been introduced to me at the British Army Equipment Exhibition at Aldershot the year before, so this was our second meeting. They had ordered 200 Mark 5 Sterling Patchett silenced sub-machine guns (L34A1), which are to this day on the standard equipment list of the British Armed Forces.

"Surely you've received delivery of these by now, Sir? They were sent to the docks and should have been shipped long before I left England," I insisted.

The Jordanians shook their heads.

"Very well. I'll Telex the factory right away to find out what's been going on and come back to you as soon as possible," I said apologetically.

This seemed to reassure them but I felt a deep sense of embarrassment.

On my way to the ship's telegraph office, I began to wonder what could have happened to the order. It started to worry me; the company had never experienced this sort of problem before. All the papers were in order. The consignment had been substantiated by export documents, including an end-user certificate signed by General Hilmi Lozi, a senior officer in the Jordanian Army. Its destination was Jordan. Sterling's works director, David Howroyd, was supposed to be handling this and he was normally very reliable. So what could possibly have gone wrong?

At the ship's telegraph office, arrangements were made for the Telex to be sent immediately. I was most curious to find out what had happened in order to get back to the general. As I made my way back to the exhibition, many thoughts were racing through my mind.

Chapter 2

The Knock

While awaiting Howroyd's response to the Telex, unknown to me, other quite different events were unfolding down at the docks back in London. A team of Customs investigation officers had swooped down on the Victoria Deep Water Terminal at Greenwich to seize and impound the shipment of 200 Sterling sub-machine guns. Though the guns had been consigned to Aqaba, Customs suspected that their ultimate destination might be Iraq, in breach of current export regulations.

Iraq was the favoured participant in the Iraq/Iran War, since the Shah had been a good customer of the British defence industry and a friend of Britain. His enemies had managed to get rid of him, and nobody liked the unpredictability of the new ultra-religious Islamic regime. The Gulf Arab states, most of them staunchly Anglophile, threw in their lot by giving support and financial aid to Iraq, although not actually providing men or arms.

Sabre-rattling is an excellent time for generating arms sales, but when hostilities actually ensue, the British Government, anxious not to fan the flames, morally forbids arms sales to either side of a conflict situation. This was now the case and whereso'er the sympathies lay, this was an irrelevance and the embargo would stand.

It must now be remembered that all the bad things that were subsequently run up against Saddam Hussein had not yet been mentioned. Nothing appeared to be known (or admitted) about his treatment of political opponents, Marsh Arabs etc., and he had not yet made any moves to invade Kuwait.

Customs International Division (ID) has a formidable and

frightening reputation for search, seizure and interrogation, as well as instilling terror in their quarry. With their far-ranging and draconian powers emanating from the days of brandy smuggling in the West Country and the collection of His Majesty's rightful revenue, to the bullying of small businesses with an overwhelming VAT bureaucracy, Customs has acquired few friends.

They jealously guard these historic powers and view their law enforcement role as paramount, with a zeal that is bordering on the evangelical. So the Customs officers involved were relishing the prospect of this sensational "knock" and later putting down more than a few jars at their headquarters at New King's Beam House to celebrate their arms catch.

The thought of a high profile interception of sub-machine guns destined for Iraq and the excitement of carrying out the raid must have been irresistible – far more appealing than policing smuggled drugs, tobacco and alcohol, and much more prestigious. Meanwhile, on Britain's streets, smuggled drugs were plentiful and billions of pounds of tax and excise were being stolen or evaded.

Having seized and impounded the consignment, Customs investigation officers then launched an operation to raid Sterling's factory in Dagenham and arrest and interview me and David Howroyd, but not before calling upon Reginald Dunk at his home in Nottinghamshire.

Dunk was the immensely likeable owner and managing director of the private arms-dealing firm Atlantic Commercial (UK) Limited, who had introduced the small Jordan order to Sterling and arranged for the end-user certificate to be forthcoming. The tall military-moustached Major Dunk was not some fly-by-night but a former property developer born in Barnsley who had been educated at an English public school – Rossall – and had been commissioned in the British Army.

Dunk and Atlantic Commercial had been introduced to me in the late 1970s, when Sterling's product range included sub-machine guns and Armalite rifles. Sterling had regularly supplied small arms to the Middle East (specifically the Gulf States), Africa and the Far East, but had no fixed agency arrangements and were happy for Dunk to act for us on an ad hoc basis in many countries. He had mentioned Iraq but I disregarded this because of the export regulations. Also, as the Soviet Union was now supplying Iraq with small arms, Iraq was of no interest to me whatsoever.

Throughout Sterling's life, Jordan had given the company irregular but substantial orders for Mark 4 and smaller quantities of Mark 5 sub-machine guns. The country had a special place in the esteem of the British Government and a "most favoured nation" trading status for military equipment. So it was not at all unreasonable to assume that the order was entirely genuine. Besides, it came not long after the British Army Equipment Exhibition where the Mark 5s had attracted attention from Jordan and had produced an enquiry. Furthermore, the two Jordanian generals whom I had met at this exhibition were well known to the British Ministry of Defence.

Hence, Jordan had a substantial holding of sub-machine guns from Sterling. This was augmented on an intermittent basis when funding allowed. In other words, the Hashemite Kingdom of Jordan, although modest in its natural resources, was, and continued to be, a most valued and favoured customer of the company.

And so it was, in the early hours of 18 February 1983, a team of burly-looking Customs men descended on Dunk's home. Furious at being roused in the early hours by a Customs "home visit", Dunk goaded them. "Yes, search whole bloody place if ya like – and don't forget Sherman fookin' tank in't barn!"

They took him at his word, leaving no paperclip unturned. So there was some disappointment on discovering that there was, in fact, no Sherman tank. Though not amused by Dunk's little jest, the Customs men did, however, find a collection of diaries and correspondence regarding Sterling's involvement in the order and a copy of a letter to me from Dunk mentioning "our beak-nosed friend Khalid the Corruptible". At the time, I had no idea who he was.

Next on the list for a visit was Alex Schlesinger, Dunk's sales consultant. Customs arrived at his home to question him about whether the Jordanian order was ever discussed with Dunk as an Iraqi deal. Schlesinger was quite co-operative and felt little hesitation in being candid about government knowledge of arms exports through Jordan to Iraq:

> Not really. We joke about these things. My reaction was, yes, a Jordanian transaction but only as a smoke screen. We know everything that goes to Jordan ends up in Iraq. Who are we to judge?

So far as Schlesinger was concerned, the British authorities were aware that diversion from Jordan was a strong possibility so why all the raids and heavy-handedness? Why grant the export licence if they had any concerns about end destination, he thought.

Having visited Dunk and Schlesinger, Customs moved on to the Sterling factory in Dagenham in order to question me. And so began a twenty-five-year saga that changed the course of my life.

But all did not go quite to plan. Had the investigators done their homework properly before barging in on Sterling, they might have discovered that I was attending the MOD's defence exhibition in Jordan at the time. There was some considerable disappointment that I was out of the country on business and unavailable for interview. Unfortunately, this did not bode well for Howroyd, the hapless works director, who unwittingly became the focus of the Customs interrogation and their shock tactics.

Howroyd was bullied by the Customs investigators. So frightening was the interrogation, that it became necessary to have our solicitors present, though Customs resented the involvement of "meddling lawyers".

Inevitably, there was some delay while Payne Hicks Beach & Co., the company's solicitors, despatched a young Australian lawyer, John Manuell, to supervise the interrogation. Manuell took pride in not appearing as the traditional stuffy Pommie lawyer and arrived on his huge Moto-Guzzi motorcycle. He was looking forward to putting the Customs investigators in their place and ensuring fair play.

Manuell's intervention had a sobering effect. The atmosphere suddenly changed for the better, though Howroyd was still shell-shocked and nervous. Eventually, after some two hours, the Customs men left.

Howroyd had been co-operative throughout and denied any knowledge that the goods were destined for Iraq. The officers had left the factory saying that they would be back soon to interview me and that I, Edmiston, shouldn't even think of travelling abroad again before they had done so – in true cop style.

It had been a busy day for the Customs men but there was still more work to be done. Enquiries followed with the Iraqi and Jordanian Embassies to investigate the destination of the goods. These interviews also did not go quite as expected.

The Iraqi response was that the goods were, in fact, destined for Jordan. The officials explained that this was a typical example of the generosity between Arab countries. In view of their good relations with Jordan, Iraq had decided to make them a gift of the Sterling sub-machine guns. This response was a bit of a surprise. Were embassy officials to give such evidence at trial, this could jeopardize the successful outcome of any prosecution, the Customs men thought.

Chapter 3

London Calling

Meanwhile, back on the floater, I was patiently awaiting a response from the factory to my Telex. While pondering the situation, a Ministry of Defence official boldly marched over to me with news that, apparently, the Saturday edition of the *Daily Express* had printed a story about Sterling and me. "Looks like the shit's hit your fan," he smirked.

I thought at first that this was some kind of joke that the lads from the other defence companies were playing on me. But this was February 1983 – too early for an April Fool.

I scanned the paper and was shocked at the report: Customs investigators had pounced on the factory; Sterling and I were now under suspicion of gunrunning; and Customs had seized the consignment at the Victoria Deep Water Terminal before shipment. The hour was too late to call the factory so there would be a wait until morning to find out more. But it was now clear enough why the generals had not received the consignment.

After a restless night I awoke early, keen for a response, so I rushed over to the telegraph office. A Telex had arrived from the factory in Dagenham. It was from David Howroyd.

"Urgent you call – but watch your language. David."

I managed to use the ship-to-shore telephone to ring back.

"David, what's going on with the Jordan order and what the hell are Customs up to?"

"Your friend Dunk has really landed us in the mire."

"What do you mean?" I was shocked.

"Well, Customs are now saying that although the consignment was being sent to Jordan, it would have ended up in Iraq. But we didn't know this and Dunk had assured us that it wasn't for Iraq."

"Just a minute, Dave," I interrupted. "That's a load of horse. I've got two bloody Jordanian generals here bleating at me 'cos their effing guns are overdue. Now you're telling me that some arsehole in Customs has stopped it, when we're paying out thousands with the MOD here to drum up export orders. Are you kidding me, or did Keith forget to pay the bloody VAT this month?"

"Watch what you say, James. It's really serious. I'm not going through another grilling with those bastards. You'd better come back and sort it out immediately. These people mean business; they're coming back to see you next and they could revoke our licence and close us down!"

"Okay, I'll be on the next plane."

So this was real. The goods had been seized and impounded and, having been down at the factory, Customs now also wanted to question me. Worse still was the harmful press publicity, as well as the thought of how customers and suppliers would react.

Chapter 4

Reflections

I had booked myself on the next flight back to London to get to the bottom of this mysterious and embarrassing matter.

Though Alia, the Royal Jordanian Airline, was comfortable and caring, my mind was troubled. The hostesses looked rather elegant and relaxed in their sand and scarlet uniforms but the calmness of this environment did little to allay my anxiety.

What was going on and where could it all lead? The events of the last twenty-four hours were still spinning around in my head: the questions from the Jordanian Army officers about the non-delivery of the order; the Ministry of Defence official informing me of the press report; and Howroyd in a state of complete panic about Customs' accusation over "Arms to Iraq". It was incredible to think that, having built the company up to its current success, its future now seemed in jeopardy.

My involvement in military small arms had started in the 1970s. They encompassed most of the manufacturing processes already at my disposal within the general engineering works I had acquired after leaving university. My interest stemmed solely from this.

As far as the moral side of gun-making is concerned, people have their own opinions. My own feelings were coloured by having watched rounds thump into the butts of shooting ranges when on target duty in the Honourable Artillery Company (HAC, Territorial Army) and on the range at Sterling. The thought of the damage that could be caused to a human body made me wince. However, I believed, and still believe, that war is the most wasteful and repellent occupation, and resort to it should be discouraged at all costs. Hence, the more terrifying, ruthless and efficient that weapons are, the more those who govern us may think twice before resorting to their use. That is the basic philosophy behind nuclear weapons, which succeeded in keeping the Cold War cold.

British industry and engineering has a long tradition of quality gun production, both military and sporting, and is well capable of supplying our own armed forces with the very best weaponry available. Homeland security – the right for a country to defend itself – is the ultimate justification and muddled thinking should not unfairly influence our police or our politicians. The moral responsibility for the actual supply of weapons to (friendly) foreign governments and their respective agencies is supposed to be taken by government.

The views of others around me, such as Sterling's chief designer who could not condone the use of firearms on birds and animals, were well-respected. The company regularly exchanged Christmas cards with those running Amnesty International and the Campaign Against the Arms Trade, however misguided some thought their views to be.

One statistic that is difficult to explain is that when small arms, particularly handguns, are outlawed, gun crime figures soar, as in Britain. In recent years in the US, gun sales, particularly military type assault rifles, have risen substantially and yet gun crime has reduced by more than twenty per cent.

Sterling had been successful and this had brought great rewards for my family. A sumptuous eight-bedroom mansion (with its own lift and sauna) on the Phillimore Estate allowed an enviable lifestyle in one of London's prime residential areas. Here, we lived just around the corner from Kensington High School, where my daughters Pandora, Portia and Scarlett attended. Being so close, they were inexcusably late every single morning.

There had been a new addition to the family the previous year – J.Harry – the son and heir. I now had a successor to groom for this empire. A dark blue Bentley was the family means of transport, from the back of which the sweet little rich girls bedecked in smocked dresses would stick their tongues out cheekily at passing motorists. Regular dinner parties with the best of food and wines flowing freely were also a feature of the Edmiston social scene.

Though most of my peer group had been successful in law, accountancy, banking or property, I had chosen to forsake my university subject – law – to pursue a passion for precision engineering. "James, you're the only person we know who makes things," they would say. But I was proud to be a British manufacturer and strongly believed that Britain's future depended on its ability to produce and export world-class goods.

Having turned around a small engineering company I had acquired after leaving Oxford, in 1971, still in my twenties, I took on the Sterling Armament Company. Sterling had manufactured in toto the world renowned Mark 4 9mm sub-machine gun (L2A3), which at that time was the standard in the British Armed Forces, as well as having been exported to more than ninety countries.

May Waller was the lady who first put me on the trail of Sterling when we "inherited" her on buying our house in Chelsea when Sisi and I were first married. Her other employer at the time was distraught when her boyfriend (the colourful Clive Raphael), who was chairman of the group of companies that included Sterling, was killed in an air crash piloting the company plane in the South of France. That was the start of the saga that has occupied my waking hours for the last forty years.

The public may have known May's son and her brother, who used to sell flowers most amiably on the steps of the Spanish Embassy in Belgrave Square before the advent of frozen Israeli flowers that are sold in supermarkets, and before the Grosvenor Estate hiked their licence fee by a factor of three.

The Sterling is still probably the most reliable automatic firearm ever made. It passed the British Army trial to ensure that it functioned not only at Antarctic temperatures, but after total immersion in water and sand. No other weapon was as successfully tested thus. In fact, the test report states that it was concluded because after 30,000 rounds, there was no appreciable wear. There was justifiable pride in its reputation for quality and supreme reliability, in whatever the terrain and weather conditions.

It had even gained media fame in at least two of the James Bond films, including *Casino Royale* and *On Her Majesty's Secret Service*. What better weapon, of course, to provide for the quintessential British spy who needs to be defended by one of the most iconic guns that Q can provide for him. Sterling had also achieved cult status through *Star Wars*, when Bapty & Co. (weaponry and props suppliers to the entertainment industry) modified the Mark 4 as the weapon of the inter-galactic storm troopers.

The Sterling's accuracy was remarkable considering the standard pistol round that it fires. In fact, its range is not far short of the ubiquitous AK-47 rifle and is also a whole kilogram lighter than its much publicized Israeli rival – the Uzi.

Its stablemate, the Sterling Mark 5 silenced gun, had been the door-opener at many live demonstrations of military equipment around the world. It was truly fantastic in that apart from being muffled with a silencer, the supersonic 9mm round had been scientifically slowed to below the speed of sound so that it was quite unrecognizable as a firearm. This, coupled with night vision equipment, offered the customer a truly awesome combination.

With the help of an utterly loyal workforce of more than 100 at Dagenham, the company's manufacturing capability had been expanded. The 5.56mm Armalite AR-18 rifle was made at Dagenham predominantly for the American civilian market. Apart from the technical knowledge acquired in making a new gun, the collaboration with Armalite had shown just what a powerful market the American civilian gun market was.

The company had developed a new long-barrelled semi-automatic Sterling for that market called the Mark 6. The Bureau of Alcohol Tobacco and Firearms had just approved it for sale in the US. A joint company had been formed with a keen young Texan called Roma Skinner to market it. The market potential was greater by far than the whole of the free world's military and police sales.

Sterling also made an air rifle that could be sold on the British civilian market. In terms of strength and accuracy, it was unparalleled, and has become a sought-after classic. A licence agreement had also been effected with J.P. Sauer & Sohn of Eckernförde, near Kiel in Germany to develop their .38" special revolver into a larger .357" magnum gun. It had a superb compensating pressure trigger mechanism and would have surely have made its presence also felt in a Clint Eastwood movie. Sterling was developing this and had already acquired special production plant. The company had also been successful in licensing a rifle of in-house design to Chartered Industries in Singapore, which was in fact a government arsenal.

There were other companies within the group; namely Yaffle Importers & Exporters Ltd, which dealt in sporting guns and accessories for the English domestic market. It was well run by Tom Kent, who had started as the driver at Sterling.

Further, there was a successful machine tool importing company (P & E Machine Tools Ltd), which only imported (Swiss, Japanese and Spanish) machine tools, the equivalent of which were not obtainable from British manufacturers.

My original firm – Paul Escaré Engineering Ltd – was particularly well equipped and was engaged in the production of scheduled parts for firms such as CAV, Perkins Engines, Rank Xerox, Aston Martin Lagonda, Mycalex of Cirencester, Smiths Industries and Barwell Engineering.

Another company – Automatic Products (Edgware) Ltd – was engaged in the ultra-high production, by cold heading, solely of hose-clip screws for the various British companies that made the hose clips themselves.

So, I had been highly successful in running companies whose reputation for quality was second to none. Virtually the entire production of Sterling was exported. Having travelled the world to promote sales, turnover was set fair to double within the next two years. But could all this now be in jeopardy? What was going on?

The goods that the Jordanian generals were chasing up had been ordered by Jordan, and the export licence application had named

Jordan as the ultimate customer. The Jordanian authorities had supplied an end-user certificate to confirm this and the British Authorities were entirely comfortable for the order to go ahead. Why, then, were Customs & Excise investigators causing such a problem, and weren't the authorities aware that Sterling was fulfilling this order through Dunk?

My first meeting with Dunk I had reported to the authorities, and no adverse comments had been made about this or the subsequent Jordanian order. The consignment was a small order for 200 Mark 5s. It had been spelled out to Dunk that had this been for Iraq, it would have been a complete waste of time as the export licence would not have been granted. Dunk assured me that the order had nothing to do with Iraq and showed me an end-user certificate on Jordanian Army notepaper signed by Hilmi Lozi. Sterling submitted this to the Department of Trade and Industry with the request for the export licence, which was granted.

I was a wholehearted supporter of the MOD Sales team (later, the Defence Export Service Organization, DESO), who were also responsible for the staging of British static and floating defence exhibitions. The name was rather inaccurate since the actual selling was left to individual companies, but their marketing and liaison with British embassies and high commissions around the globe was superb. True, MOD Sales would attempt to sell the products of the Royal Ordnance Factories, but they would also give every assistance to any British company dealing in that euphemism, "defence equipment".

They would tacitly accept any export licence refusals as laid down by the Department of Trade and Industry – ultimately relying on the Foreign and Commonwealth Office (FCO) for the final sanction. But they spared absolutely no effort to assist right up to that point.

Having relied upon advice from the Ministry of Defence and the Department of Trade and Industry (DTI), as well as others about British export policy, and having previously exported to Jordan, I was not expecting any issues to arise on this order. But the shipment for Jordan had been seized because it was suspected that it was going via Jordan to Iraq.

On first arriving at the port of Aqaba in February 1983, I was rather surprised that the Jordanian and Iraqi enclosures were next to each other but, no doubt, the British authorities were aware of this and it was not a concern. Some of the goods were British and plainly destined for Iraq because they were painted in Iraqi not Jordanian Army colours.

I tried to relax for the remainder of the flight. After arrival at Heathrow on a cold and bleak February morning, I rushed home to freshen up before driving down to Dagenham to investigate what hopefully would be the proverbial storm in a teacup.

Chapter 5

Falklands Arms Swoop

The reception back home was not quite as expected.

"What in God's name have you been up to?" bellowed my wife, Sisi, waving a newspaper at me. Hardly the warm welcome home I'd expected, but her concern about the Customs raid was understandable.

"Just what the hell are you talking about?" I retorted.

"Well, you've been accused in the press of gunrunning, haven't you?"

"What? We've certainly done nothing like that. I don't know what Customs are playing at."

"Then read this!" A copy of the *Daily Express* was duly thrust in front of me.

Falklands Arms Swoop: 3 quizzed
Fears that British dealers illegally shipped arms to Argentina during the Falklands crisis were being investigated by Customs officers last night. Three dealers came under suspicion after investigators swooped on a ship in Greenwich dock, London, and seized 200 Sterling sub-machine guns bound for Iraq. Arms shipments to Iraq are banned in Britain.... Last night three men were being questioned about the shipment, which was due to leave for Iraq via Cyprus tomorrow. A former senior Army officer is one of them, along with his son.... Customs investigators were also seeking to interview the managing director of Sterling, who is believed to be out of the country on business....

This cheap sensationalist bit of inaccurate journalese was really appalling. Doubtless it had been inspired by Customs and Excise as part of their disruption policy. But my real concern was the insinuation of treachery during the Falklands War. Such a terrible slur on my good name and Sterling's reputation could ruin us. Worse still, it could endanger my family.

The true position was quite different. The British Government had authorized both these orders. The Argentine order had been executed with their full approval at least two years before the Falklands crisis. So what were Customs up to and why?

It all seemed very odd to me. The government had been very keen to support the British armament industry and promote British military exports worldwide. Such exports also helped to protect that industry in the essential role of homeland security. This was conspicuously absent from the article, no doubt, in order to avoid spoiling a sensationalist scoop with the facts.

Sterling had derived much satisfaction from exporting top quality British-made goods to Argentina and Jordan with complete government approval. The Mark 5 silenced sub-machine gun had undergone extensive trials with the Argentine Naval Commandos – the absolute elite corps of Argentina's armed forces. The Argentinians had bought Sterlings simply because they were the best.

Though the company and I were utterly innocent of gunrunning, my wife prattled on about what our family and friends would think about the article and the implication that Sterling and I had been unpatriotic. Her particular concern was the welfare of the children. How could they show their faces at school when their peers would taunt them about having a traitor as a father?

In a fury, I dived into the Bentley and tore off to Dagenham at top speed. A motorcycle policeman stopped me on A13 and booked me for speeding at 96mph; I was just desperate to find out what the devil was going on.

En route, the damaging article was uppermost in my mind. The arms trade is one of utmost trust and respectability and transgressors of the rules are visibly shunned by all. This news would travel quickly – very quickly. The publicity would cause acute embarrassment to government departments like MOD Sales and defence attachés in embassies and high commissions around the globe. Everyone would have to immediately distance themselves from me and the company – we could soon be ruined.

On arrival in the office, it was clear that the staff were also worried. The first thing was to speak with the works director, David Howroyd, and Keith Cole, the company accountant. They were still reeling in shock after the Customs interviews and were glad to see me back.

After this briefing, it was important to go round the factory to reassure the employees about the Customs visit and that their jobs were safe. All sorts of rumours were flying around but they were told not to attach too much importance to the *Express* report and the raid. Fortunately, it was common knowledge that the Argentine order had pre-dated the war, with full government approval. The loyal workforce was utterly supportive and relieved.

Now that things were settling down a little at the factory, there was time to focus on sorting out the *Express* report in order to reassure customers and contacts. Were our bankers, the Bank of Scotland, also to find out about this, there was a real danger they could close the account. Finding a replacement in such adverse circumstances would not be easy.

I decided that it was best to tell the bank about the report and ask for a chance to obtain a retraction and an apology. They agreed. However, defamation cases often drag on and are always a crippling expense. Without an immediate apology, the company could have been finished. The pressure to achieve a satisfactory resolution was intense.

During my absence while I was in Jordan, Keith Cole had instructed Payne Hicks Beach to write to the *Express* correcting the numerous inaccuracies and demanding an immediate retraction with a full apology. A copy of the letter was posted on the company notice board to allay any fears. It read:

Dear Sirs,

We refer to an article printed on page 2 of the *Daily Express* on Saturday, 19 February, headed "Falklands Arms Swoop: 3 quizzed" by Michael O'Flaherty.

The facts recited in relation to our clients are incorrect....

Our clients are long-established and highly-reputable manufacturers of small arms and deeply resent the smear which that article, by false association, casts on them. Our clients are not arms dealers, and have no part in illegal supply of arms to Argentina or elsewhere, nor any other illegality. They are in fact accustomed to working in close association with all relevant agencies of HM Government.

As for "200 Sterling SMGs bound for Iraq ... via Cyprus," these weapons were ordered for the Armed Forces of Jordan, and were bound directly for Aqaba, Jordan, pursuant to the Export Licence granted by the Board of Trade, and as the shipping documents verify.

As for "the managing director of Sterling, who is believed to be out of the country on business," Mr James Edmiston is, as is well known, representing the company on a British Government-sponsored Military Trade Exhibition presently touring the Arab States.

Payne Hicks Beach had advised that there was no guarantee of early settlement. We could end up fighting a national newspaper in the High Court with all the attendant expense and damaging publicity. Sterling certainly had enough to contend with defending the Customs prosecution without the spectre of having to fund a libel action as well.

Fortunately, it was not necessary to go legal. The *Express* agreed to publish an unreserved apology: a correction was printed and they paid legal costs. More importantly, the settlement also meant that the bank did not close the account. But the damage had been done to Sterling's reputation. However, I now had to focus on the Customs investigation in order to save myself and the company.

Chapter 6

Friendly Words

While busy calming things down, unknown to me, events were unfolding back at New King's Beam House. Senior Customs investigation officers were preparing to have a few quiet, friendly words with the Iraqi and Jordanian Embassies to get the story straight.

Because the officers were concerned about what the embassies had said about the Jordan order and how this could jeopardize the case if a jury accepted it they were taking no chances. The stakes were high and an enormous amount of work had already been carried out at great public expense. It might not look so good for Customs and HMG if the case were aborted now or was unsuccessful at trial.

Customs also had to keep the Foreign Office closely informed given the sensitive diplomatic factors. And, of course, the Foreign Office had to be kept closely informed about the visits to the embassies in order to maintain good relations with Iraq and Jordan.

So, on 25 February 1983, Mr Knox, Assistant Chief Investigation Officer at Customs, sent a letter to Mr Patrick Wogan at the Foreign Office concerning the visits to the Iraqi and Jordanian Embassies. The letter reported:

> You asked for a copy of my officers' reports concerning their visits to the Iraqi and Jordanian Embassies. These are enclosed.
>
> You will see that, given time, the two embassies have put their heads together and produced a united front with a story that is neither credible nor supported by the documentary and oral evidence we now possess.

My only concern is the possible effect this story may have in future criminal proceedings should the defence lawyers decide to obtain the agreement of the embassy personnel to appear as witnesses. It may be prudent for us to confront the ambassadors with the contradictory evidence in our possession before such an eventuality becomes fact in the hope that it will deter them from taking a potentially embarrassing course of action.

I am reviewing the strength of our evidence at the moment and before we take any firm decisions on the diplomatic side I may wish to discuss this aspect of the investigation with you.

Dunk and I, our lawyers and the court were unaware of this letter and report and the plot "to confront the ambassadors … in the hope that it will deter them from taking a potentially embarrassing cause of action" until it was unearthed by Lord Justice Scott *ten* years later, in 1993.

Chapter 7

Dilemma

Now that the libel case was out of the way, we could turn our full attention to the investigation.

I thought it advisable to consult Major Keen and David Howroyd about what to do next. Major Bernard Bevan Keen RM was the recently retired sales director who had been with the company for some twenty years after an illustrious career as a marine officer. He had at one time been the senior marine aboard HMS *Belfast*, and had always specialized in small arms. He used to wear a battered trilby when driving, in order to protect his bald pate in the event of an accident. However, when I jokingly stated that my father-in-law had condemned all hatted drivers as being unpredictable, the brown trilby was seen no more.

Major Keen and David Howroyd were also baffled as to why the authorities were acting in this way given that they had been kept informed and had granted the licence. We were all most concerned about the serious allegations and the potential effects on the company.

Meanwhile, the thought had struck me that, if the manufacturing licence was withdrawn, the company was finished. If I were to end up with a criminal record, more than 100 loyal employees would be out of work, with all that that entailed for their families. Furthermore, with a criminal record, I would not be able to cash in on the bounty that was on the horizon in the shape of the US arms market.

It was a good month before the Customs investigators arrived down at Sterling to interview me. The interview was courteous, and nothing much transpired. I reinforced my belief in the bona fides of the order for Jordan by giving an account of my meetings with the Jordanian generals.

Customs and Excise were overly interested in the reference picked up in the copy of a letter from Dunk to me about "our beak-nosed friend, Khalid the Corruptible". I had never heard of Khalid. Who was he? Customs could not believe that I did not know him; they told me that Khalid was one Khalid Rahal, who worked at the Iraqi Embassy. But Dunk's flowery turn of phrase was certainly entertaining and I had scarcely taken it seriously.

We were hoping that the investigation would be dropped. Knowing that I was now on my own and potentially in a serious fix, it was time to consult the lawyers again.

The company used Payne Hicks Beach because I had been at school, university and in the Territorial Army (HAC) with one of the partners, Anthony Slingsby. Slingsby was a large, balding man, always more mature than his years. Having been president of the Oxford University Conservative Association, his undoubted ambition was to become President of the Law Society. He had an unconscious habit of mimicking his heroine, Margaret Thatcher, which slightly irritated me. My American friends liked Slingsby enormously. Their name for him, "Tony Baby", stuck with those at Sterling who knew him.

I should mention that Slingsby had, once before, saved my bacon. When I was at school, four of us were packed off to a chateau in the Loire region of France. The chateau was impressive but had certainly seen better days, as it was dropping apart and had not seen a paintbrush since the Third Empire. The old widowed Comtesse Choulot de Thauvenay was much the same. Although cultured and well-spoken, she looked more the fearsome peasant than aristocrat.

To celebrate our arrival, on the first evening of our two-week stay we cycled into the local village, which was perched on top of a steep hill, and had a few beers at the bistro. Did I say a few? Probably a few too many would be more of an understatement. My friend Maurice Cowin, later to be an officer in the Royal Navy, fell off his bike and split his chin. He bled like a sacrificial pig. So much so that he left a giveaway trail to the bedroom we were sharing. The next day, Madame la Comtesse blew her top.

"How dare Rugby School send over such badly-behaved drunken hooligans!" We were ordered to depart forthwith. What would the school do to us? Rugby town had at that time the great distinction of having more pubs per head of population than any other town in England. But as far as the school was concerned, having a snort was an expellable offence.

Old Slingsby (even then he was mature) drew himself up to his 6ft 4ins, put his arm around the shoulder of the Comtesse, and in a torrent of fluent French, albeit with the strongest English accent, elaborated in great detail on the small amount we had consumed and that the accident had been occasioned by the presence of mud on the road. The Comtesse simply did not believe this yarn and so we were called upon to prove it. We cycled back to the village, with the Comtesse struggling to keep up in her aged 2 CV car. To this day, I cannot believe what I saw. There, was a pile of horse manure in the very place where Maurice had parted company with his bike.

All was forgiven; Slingsby was our real hero. When we arrived back at the chateau, I looked up at the large painting of the late Comte, fully bearded and resplendent in the uniform of a French general, complete with dark red kepi, and I could have sworn that he winked at me.

And so it was important to retain Payne Hicks Beach to handle the Customs case. I could completely trust Slingsby, and they were the company's regular lawyers. But the case was bound to be a little more challenging than persuading the Comtesse of our innocence. Though Slingsby was concerned for his friend, he still had to look after the interests of the firm. In common with many other senior partners, he was under pressure to maximize his billings. It was amusing to see him activate his chess clock to indicate the social niceties were over and that time was now chargeable.

But Payne Hicks Beach was not the kind of firm of solicitors that dealt with anything other than "blue chip" clients and, in fact, did not in the normal course of events handle any criminal work. There was a certain sense of unease at Payne Hicks Beach about becoming involved with such a high profile criminal case involving alleged arms dealing and the effect it could have on their firm – quite understandably. However, the firm was convinced that we were completely innocent and felt it was their duty to stand by us.

The advice was quite worrying. If an offence had been committed then, at best, the goods could be forfeited and there could be a fine of up to £88,000. At worst, I could be facing up to two years' imprisonment. That was quite apart from the revocation of any licences or manufacturing permits for the future, which would have put the company out of business. In view of this, I was now concerned to find out more about the Customs investigation and the likely outcome for us.

Slingsby was very helpful, though it was necessary for Sterling to pay some £5,000 on account – a small fortune in those days – but as it turned out, there was a lot of work to do. John Manuell was given the job. He was indeed a fine choice, but it was Slingsby, now utterly incredulous, who spelt out to me just how serious things had become.

Chapter 8

Keeping Sterling Afloat

In view of the publicity in the *Daily Express*, I was continuing to keep the company's bankers informed of the Customs investigation in order to give them some reassurance. At the same time, I was also in the middle of buying in a large minority of the outstanding shares in Sterling. The bank's help was needed in financing the purchase of this shareholding, and, needless to say, they were not over-enthusiastic about continuing their support if there was any risk of prosecution that could jeopardize the company.

Slingsby also thought it prudent to keep the company's accountants abreast of developments. The accountants were Messrs Arthur Young McClelland Moores and the partner in charge was the affable Tim (AD) Chessells. He had been handling the Sterling account for several years and his advice was invaluable. His other "interesting" client at the time had been the bullion firm Johnson Matthey, from whom Sterling bought their silver solder for induction brazing operations.

Slingsby and Chessells advised that it would be a good idea for the whole matter to be considered and quantified as to potential loss. They advised that it was necessary to place a contingency on the company accounts in relation to the pending case and potential penalties.

It was now more than two months since the seizure and the initial interviews and we still had no idea what Customs would do. I needed to know in order to make important business decisions. Slingsby suggested that an experienced counsel's opinion should be sought and that Robin Auld QC was the man for the job. He was a leading criminal defence lawyer with vast experience of Customs cases. A conference was arranged with him for 28 April 1983.

Time passed by very quickly and I soon found myself down at chambers in the Temple for a conference with Auld. Accompanied by Howroyd, Cole and Manuell, we were all nervous, not knowing quite what to expect, having been warned that a custodial sentence could not be ruled out. I was very conscious of the gravity of the situation and the potential seriousness of the matter. Having never had more than a speeding ticket, this was an intimidating experience that I could never have imagined.

Auld was measured and authoritative. We explained all about the order and that it was meant for Jordan. Though Auld and Manuell were supportive, I wondered what a jury would make of all of this. Auld advised that though he was confident of our innocence, they might just see it as "arms dealing", regardless.

The advice was that, if convicted, a prison sentence was unlikely but the fine could be as much as £300,000 – not much of a consolation, really. I needed to know where I stood as soon as possible. Auld said that he would speak to Customs immediately to find out the position. Perhaps a solution could be found to minimize the damage.

Yet it was another two months before Auld was eventually able to speak with Customs, in June. The disappointing upshot was that Customs were unwilling to drop the case. Apparently, the Commissioners took a very serious view of arms exports to the Middle East. Their general policy was to prosecute such cases in order to discourage others, and they were especially likely to do so in this case, given the *Daily Express* article. But curiously, the papers had not yet been submitted to Customs' Solicitors' Office for advice. I wondered why their solicitors were being kept in the dark and how this could affect me.

Chapter 9

Der Prozess

The news from Auld was a real concern. Obsessed by the worry that the bank might appoint a receiver, I just had to see if there was a solution that might avoid this. In desperation, I made an appointment in July with the Customs case officers, Messrs Byrne and Matthews, with John Manuell present to see if compounding was a possibility. Decisions had to be made for all sorts of obvious reasons.

The weekend before the meeting, I tried to relax by watching the Wimbledon Men's Singles Final. John McEnroe had reached his fourth consecutive final, dropping only one set throughout the whole championship and beating the unknown New Zealander, Chris Lewis, in straight sets. At the Customs meeting, although the officers appeared to be receptive and helpful, I had the utmost difficulty in resisting the temptation to invoke McEnroe's famous plea, "You cannot be serious!" However, they gave me the name of a Mr Silverstone of the Policy Department and suggested it would be worth making an appointment with him.

A meeting with a rotund, pale, dead-pan Silverstone took place some two days later. There were no surprises. He stated that the investigation would take a further two to three months – possibly more – to finish. The investigation was incomplete and neither he nor anyone else was in a position to say whether or not there would be a prosecution.

The meeting, which had taken place in a huge executive office, had started unusually at one o'clock in the afternoon, and had been singularly unhelpful. The outcome, Manuell advised me, was that a prosecution now seemed likely. He would have to start preparing our defence and calculate the contingent liability if the outcome was unfavourable.

There was little choice other than to inform the bank and the accountants. An appointment was made to visit the head of the Bank of Scotland, Andrew Davidson – the living embodiment of a canny Scot – in the bank's elaborate offices in Threadneedle Street. The bank had already prejudged the case. The stern Davidson reluctantly, but fairly, allowed me three months until September to sort it all out. By then, Sterling was expected to have found alternative banking facilities. A contingent liability was placed on Sterling's accounts of up to £100,000 if the outcome was unfavourable.

I was livid at having to undergo the ignominy of a criminal investigation when innocent. The whole ethos of the company had been one of utmost co-operation with the authorities and the police. Sterling had always enjoyed a good relationship with the police and, ironically, often advised them on firearms prosecutions.

Chapter 10

Storm Clouds Gathering

Finding alternative banking facilities was not proving a simple task.

In the end, it was decided to sell Sterling. The likelihood of a prosecution and its possible consequences, especially the loss of the prohibited weapons manufacturing licence (Section 5), was too serious. However, the agreed purchase of the outstanding shares in the group had to be completed first before a buyer could be found. My main concern was that there would be some security for the loyal workforce. It was like a nightmare that had turned into reality.

Sterling had been successfully built up over some twelve years. Having acquired total ownership, I was then to be faced with selling the company quickly at a value much discounted from its true worth because of pending criminal charges and the consequential contingency on the balance sheet. In short, my pride in the company, its products and its employees was to be tested to the ultimate by having to sell it to limit any further damage.

A few prospective buyers were wheeled in and, eventually, Sterling was sold. The successful buyer, a gun enthusiast with an accountancy qualification, was presented to Stephen Adamson, the corporate recovery partner at Arthur Young's, who was not that enthusiastic. The sale, however, took an inordinate amount of professional time in a lawyers' contest between Freshfields and Payne Hicks Beach. The deal finally went through on 22 October 1983, mere hours before my fortieth birthday. This meant that I had distanced myself from Sterling, thus protecting it and its employees from the pending prosecution.

Sterling and I had now parted, and though it was in everyone's best interests, I was more than extremely regretful. It had been a happy and successful private company; most of the employees preferred to work there rather than down the road at Fords, where pay and career prospects may have been better. In 1983, for instance, there were six members of the Wallace family working at Sterling. The shop steward, Tom Newton, had always been friendly, straightforward and downright helpful in wage negotiation; he could see that the overriding factor for both his members and the management was the welfare of the company.

I had travelled the world representing Sterling. It was both interesting and exciting and never a hardship. Apart from pure selling, I had been invited to see how other small arms manufacturers went about their business, and had never ceased to learn new tricks of the trade. To own a successful company that made a world-renowned top quality product – and British, to boot – in its entirety was incredibly satisfying and a source of great pride.

But now I had been stripped of all this. By the time the monies had been paid off and the various outstanding debts and expenses cleared, little was left for me. But at least the company and employees would not be dragged down with me. It was left in apple-pie order. Naturally, I was extremely sad at no longer being part of it, but the real tragedy was that the company was on the verge of achieving greater success with new products and markets – especially in the US – and I would not be able to share that achievement.

There had been significant investment in new plant like CNC machinery, special-purpose machines and the superb Churchill P5 double-carriage copy lathe that had been made in Bladon by one of Britain's leading manufacturers, Matrix Churchill. I felt like I was in a void, a black hole.

Quite apart from the Customs case, there were several post-sale issues, and commissions due were never received. This led to litigation and became another unwelcome and costly diversion during a difficult period. So for me, 1983 was hardly the vintage year of all time; it was perhaps one of the worst of my life. Though it had opened with so much promise and the prospect of gaining total ownership of Sterling to achieve my long-term business plans, it had ended on a very sour note indeed with the sale, and my future was now looking perilous.

Chapter 11

Before the Beak

It had been hoped that, after losing the company in October, things would somehow improve in the New Year. But it was not to be. Things were not looking too good financially, either.

After the enforced sale of Sterling, I had become a self-employed consultant for the company, but because the commissions due never materialized I was left without any source of income. As a family man with considerable responsibilities, my debts and expenses resulted in great hardship.

With the possibility of a criminal trial hanging over my head, my marketability as an employee was not exactly enhanced. Prospective employers would not be too interested in taking on a former small arms manufacturer awaiting trial at the Old Bailey for serious alleged export offences concerning Iraq – or, in the popular idiom, gunrunning.

The first anniversary of the arrests fell in late February 1984 without incident. The Customs case had gone quiet and I had begun to hope that the prospect of a prosecution would recede with each passing day. So I tentatively started looking around for potential opportunities that would be little affected even if a prosecution were to take place.

Given the history of Sterling, my best (and only) prospect of remuneration was to continue as my own boss. The plan was to purchase another production engineering business with its own products in an area with which I was familiar and where the sale of Sterling would have little impact. But then, in April, there was an unexpected telephone call from Manuell.

"G'day James. Sorry to bother you but some bad news, I'm afraid."

"Slingsby elected President of the Law Society?" I mused.

"No, not that bad but I'm afraid Customs are going ahead after all."

"What! After fourteen months? You have to be joking!"

"Sorry, mate, but you'd better come in and see me."

I did not greet this news at all well. In fact, it was a real setback.

The reality for me, Howroyd, Sterling and others, including Dunk and Schlesinger, was that we had been charged with several arms export offences. We were all summonsed to appear at the Greenwich Magistrates' Court on 21 May. We were charged with four offences: two offences under the Export of Goods (control) order contrary to section 1 (1) Criminal Law Act 1977; and two offences under the Export of Goods (control) order contrary to Section 68 (2) Customs and Excise Management Act 1979.

The prosecution of Sterling, me and Howroyd for something we did not do was galling. Our defence was that we had made a simple application for an export licence to ship a small quantity of sub-machine guns to a friendly country – Jordan. The application was truthful and not disguised in order to mislead (compared with other companies where the DTI advice was to emphasize "general military use"). It did not need to be misleading; economy with the truth was simply not a factor for Sterling.

The main part of my defence was clear. It simply would not have been in Sterling's interest to break the law. Quite apart from the excellent reputation, which we were always at pains to preserve, there was the lack of adequate inducement. This case centred on a mere 200 guns, which never could have provided the sort of return to induce anyone to circumvent the law, especially given the potential in the US market that we were anticipating. Another important point was the destination of the consignment. If the Jordanians had been trying to buy the goods for the Iraqis, there was no way that Sterling could be expected to know.

There was every right to suppose that the British authorities had issued the export licence believing that everything was in order. If they had suspected collusion between Iraq and Jordan, it was they, not Sterling, who had acted improperly in allowing the sale to go ahead and then to prosecute innocent businessmen. This was to become a recurrent theme in the arms prosecutions that followed, especially in the Matrix Churchill case.

The Sterling business relied upon a good relationship with the police and certain government departments. It was manufacturing small arms, not machine tools. The issues were straightforward, and any refusal to grant an export licence was never questioned by the company when the government chose not to furnish an explanation.

There were a number of preliminary matters to be dealt with during 1984 arising from the charges, and eventually a committal took place at the Marylebone Magistrates' Court on 17 December. However, no date was set for the trial and I was left in limbo for yet another indefinite period. It was during this period that I decided to go ahead into an area that I knew well – guns, but non-military guns.

I had been friendly with Jim Miller, the chairman of Harris & Sheldon. He owned a well-known subsidiary called Webley & Scott, based in Birmingham, which had made handguns, shotguns and airguns in the past. Their production was now limited to airguns. Miller had indicated to me that he would sell the company at a reasonable price as its performance, although steady, was not startling.

There was also another Birmingham company, called BSA Guns, which made airguns, hunting and target rifles, and had actually produced a few sniper rifles for Sterling. I had the long-term idea of acquiring both companies, keeping their styling and marketing apart, but consolidating the manufacture of airguns. The big deterrent had been the logistical prospect of running a company in Birmingham.

However, circumstances caused me to approach Dennis Poore, the chairman of Manganese Bronze Holdings, owners of BSA Guns. Poore lived around the corner from me, in Phillimore Gardens. The circumstances were that all appeared to be quiet on the prosecution front; and I had been left with the ownership of Lanchester, in Texas, formed to sell the Mark 6 in the US, but now with nothing more to offer there.

The new owners of Sterling were concerned to stabilize the company and concentrate on core business, especially with the possible spectre of prosecution hanging over them. Unfortunately, because of this, Sterling was unable to take advantage of my plans for the US civilian market.

My American friend, Roma Skinner, was enthusiastic about BSA, which was virtually unrepresented there. He had forecast a slowly emerging market for good quality airguns but, more importantly, had carried out an in-depth market survey for hunting rifles, which, if BSA made cosmetic changes to their stuffy but good quality products, could fly, after a little time for promotion.

I was able to buy BSA by selling my Phillimore Place mansion and buying a smaller house around the corner in Argyll Road instead. The purchase duly went ahead in March 1985, at which time the trial date was unknown. I began launching new products into BSA and instigated immediately a much higher standard of polished finish on all the BSA airguns and hunting rifles.

That was all I was able to reform at the time. Customs then suddenly gave notice of a hearing on 30 September 1985 to fix the trial. And then, quite unexpectedly, the trial was set down for a very early hearing starting on 5 November.

The early date of the trial came as a complete surprise to me given that it was listed as a four-week trial. That meant there was little time to make alternative arrangements to manage the business in Birmingham from September to November. Changes to the administration and work ethic at BSA were needed but these now had to be shelved until after the trial. Though arrangements were made for BSA to be managed by others during my absence, I was out of commission for three months and the survival of the company was thrown into the balance.

Chapter 12

Incommunicado

The time after the hearing on 30 September was a critical period, requiring us to spend literally days at a time with John Manuell and an excellent barrister called David Barnard, who was quiet, modest and thorough.

There was a series of pre-trial conferences, during which proofs of evidence were reviewed and amended several times. I was earning hardly any money and the new owners of Sterling rather unwisely washed their hands of David Howroyd, claiming that the prosecution was not their problem. Obviously the two defences were going to be exactly the same, so I covered Howroyd's costs as well.

Slingsby was as good as his word on keeping the criminal defence costs to a minimum. He agreed with me that the defence could take no half measures. The damage had been done, and the future of a good name and protecting the family were the all-important issues.

Counsel advised that it would be advisable to obtain a witness statement from Major Keen about the order process at Sterling and to confirm that it complied with the regulations and that it was followed. Further, I wanted him to confirm how he unhesitatingly had introduced me to all his contacts.

Keen, who was on the board of the company until he retired in 1981, had been responsible for dealing with orders and had explained the system to me when I bought Sterling. It was a rigorous system, which I stuck to at all times.

I had always wanted to call him as a witness. He had been a brilliant salesman. No, he was not the slick, pushy type who had cut his teeth on fast-moving consumer goods, nor was he some high-flying MBA graduate, but rather in the manner of the fast disappearing 'old school'. It is generally accepted that a major of marines is the equivalent of a half-colonel in the army.

Keen was imbued with that solid British armed force tradition, and as a small arms expert, knew his subject matter to an encyclopaedic level. He did not flout this knowledge, but quietly answered and advised on any question put to him. He instilled a confidence in all with whom he dealt, and was universally liked and respected. In short, he taught me all I knew about small arms and how to sell them.

There was no hesitation whatever in his providing a witness statement. He confirmed that we had a good working relationship and that I took his advice and listened to him. Details were provided of the order process, that it complied with the regulations and that I followed it. He regarded it as his clear duty to report anything to the authorities that did not seem right, although that seldom happened. He emphasized that it was extremely rare when we received any kind of order that looked suspect.

Most of our business was directly with governments or government organizations or the Crown Agents. In particular, we kept close liaison with the Defence Sales organization, an arm of the Ministry of Defence.

He had been introduced by Defence Sales to a person in some government department whose function he was not quite aware of but assumed was some sort of intelligence. Meetings were usually held in a central London hotel so that they were aware of the company's activities and the co-operation was appreciated.

Keen had provided an extremely useful witness statement in October 1985 and we were now really counting on him to come to court to testify for us.

Co-defendants often liaise together but Manuell had warned me not to contact Dunk. It was thought that the authorities were really out to destroy him and that association with him was already damaging enough. This was quite apart from the fact that, apparently, his telephones were bugged.

I needed no prompting to have nothing further to do with Dunk. It had been made clear to him from the outset that we could not and would not have dealings with Iraq. Though he had landed me in the excrement, there was absolutely no point in open hostility between us as the damage was done. So I just hung back and kept my ears open.

On 30 September 1985, there was a hearing at the Old Bailey for pleas to be taken. All defendants pleaded not guilty and the case was adjourned for trial on 4 November. More importantly, Dunk and Schlesinger gave notice of their intention to rely on the embassy witnesses to confirm the gift defence.

Although Iraq had ordered and was paying for the order, they were doing so in order to make a gift to Jordan. This was nothing unusual. The gift was made to quote one of Dunk's letters as "a little payment as a token of their continuing friendship...."

Sir Basil Rhodes, Dunk's solicitor, was assured by the Iraqi and Jordanian Embassies that the goods were a present to the Jordanian Army. Further assurances were given in January, February, July and October 1985 that witnesses would be made available from both embassies to confirm the story in court.

Chapter 13

The Plot Thickens

With a trial fixed for November, Customs had less than five weeks to prepare their case and there was no time to lose.

Customs ID was particularly concerned that the defendants would be calling members of the Iraqi and Jordanian Embassies as witnesses for the defence and that they were still willing to appear. So, unknown to me until some ten years later, Customs decided to have a few friendly words with the Foreign Office.

As these witnesses were unlikely to assist the prosecution case, Cassey, of Customs, approached Boyce at the Foreign Office about the situation. So, on 1 October, the day after the pre-trial review, he telephoned Boyce, who recorded the call as follows:

1. HM Customs and Excise had held a pre-trial review on 30 September. The defence said that the accused would all be pleading not guilty and would be calling members of the embassy staff from both embassies as witnesses for the defence.

2. Customs and Excise said that the evidence so far presented by the embassy personnel was conflicting. If they waived their immunity and were prepared to stand as witnesses, then they would have to withstand cross-examination as well. Given HM Customs and Excise' belief that the result of this cross-examination could be potentially embarrassing to both embassies, it was Mr Cassey's view that the interests of the embassies would not be served by members of the embassies' staff agreeing to appear for the defence.

Boyce sent a copy of the note to Harding at the Foreign Office, who then had a "friendly word" with the Iraqi Ambassador about immunity, noting that, "I have passed on the thought to the Iraqi Embassy and have told Mr Cassey of our action. Both the ambassador and the First Secretary are now gone – so there is no chance of the embassy helping."

With the Iraqi witnesses now safely out of the way, the officials turned their attention to the Jordanians, but Pigott – a Foreign Office desk officer for Jordan – thought it best to clear his lines first with his superior, Nixon, stating: "I am not sure that we need to make the same noises to the Jordanians ... but if you think it appropriate I could have a word with Counsellor Kadi."

When Nixon received this, his first reaction, naturally, was reluctance. Such a course of action would impede the course of justice and if the defence ever found out, there could be consequences. But nevertheless, permission was given, and this is when Nixon told Pigott: "I confess to innocent reluctance to connive at impeding the course of justice! But you might gently enquire when talking to Kadi on other business."

"Spoke to Mr Kadi, who was grateful and agreed with C and E's advice," responded Pigott.

So, job done – the officials had succeeded in stopping the embassy witnesses from attending the trial to give evidence for the defendants.

Dunk and I were totally unaware of this "conniving at impeding the course of justice" until it was unearthed by Lord Justice Scott in 1993.

Chapter 14

At the Bailey

The five-week period leading up to the trial raced by and I was completely swallowed up by trial preparation and incessant meetings at New Square and Gray's Inn. It reminded me of the enduring old Mexican curse of "may your life be full of lawyers."

We had been depending on Major Keen to come to court to testify for us. I had hoped that he would relate how he had instructed me in the processing of an order from quotation, through acceptance, to the submission of all the correct documentation to the government department concerned. I wanted him to show how we had followed this exact procedure that he had laid down. Further, I wanted him to confirm how he unhesitatingly had introduced me to all his contacts.

However, in the seeming tradition of the service, he was a heavy smoker, and emphysema had already taken its toll. By the time of the trial, he was too ill to travel and attend court. This was a huge blow to us losing such a crucial witness. His evidence was fundamental to our defence and he would have made such a credible witness.

I was truly apprehensive of going to court. My only other previous experience of appearing before a tribunal was in my rugby playing days.

I was captaining the HAC (Honourable Artillery Company) side in the preliminary rounds of the Middlesex Sevens. I tackled one member of the opposing team possibly slightly late but was already committed. The fact that I had flattened the player after he had rid himself of the ball obviously annoyed him somewhat. So much so that he hacked me across the shin with his heel. I was never a "dirty" player, but retaliated by hoofing him in the soft part of his buttock just to show what I thought but not meaning to inflict pain. The ref saw the final part of this contretemps and sent me off.

Matters were aggravated in the dressing room afterwards when the ref asked who the team captain was. One of our players, David Chisnall, who has stretched his rugby playing over six decades ending with the Richmond "Heavies", wickedly encouraged every member of the side to claim the dubious honour of captaincy, in true Spartacus style. The ref, a Briton from over the far side of the Severn Bridge, lacked his fellow countrymen's sense of humour.

The net result was that I was summoned to appear before the RFU (Rugby Football Union) at a disciplinary hearing held at the East India and Sporting Club in St James's Square. I was detailed to present myself with the club captain (me, so that was easy) and the club president, the venerable Archie Nathan. Old Archie, full of good intent, just bumbled through how I'd played rugby from an early age, had been educated at the home of rugby, how my father had been a rugby player of renown etc., at all of which I just cringed with embarrassment.

"Well, he should have jolly well known better. He is banned for three months," was the committee's immediate decision. Notably, there was no right of appeal.

It showed me how something trivial had got completely out of hand. Could the selfsame thing happen to me before a real court of law?

It was a gruelling and tedious process having to go through all the detail day after day, along with the interminable questioning. This was a dress rehearsal, where the lawyers played devil's advocate in order to prepare the client for the rigours of cross-examination in order to make a favourable impression on the jury. Though the lawyers knew their brief well and were confident of success, they were taking no chances. Their main concern was that the prosecution would portray me as an "arms dealer", which would be highly prejudicial to the jury. It was.

Back home, my wife was supportive and tried to put a brave face on the situation. It was, of course, typical gallows humour. She joked that, if I were to be convicted and imprisoned, she would bake one of her Christmas cakes for me with a file in it. (Sisi, now with the help of our three daughters, runs a business making the finest Christmas cakes that money can buy.) Though it was a serious situation, we did our level best to make as light of it as possible.

On the morning of the trial, I woke up early and went for a run to clear my head. It was a fine autumn day and the run around Hyde Park was, in a way, mentally relaxing. Breakfast was a quiet affair as we focused on the day ahead. The doorbell rang to announce that the taxi had arrived to take us to the Old Bailey.

As the taxi made its way along Kensington High Street towards Hyde Park Corner, the atmosphere became tense and Sisi was apprehensive.

"James, I'm really worried now – what are we going to do if it goes badly? We've already lost the business, we're up to our necks in debt and now we could lose the house."

"Sisi, I keep telling you, the authorities approved the order and Dunk's got some witnesses coming from the embassies to say that the goods were for Jordan, so don't worry – it'll be alright," I replied, trying to assume a calm and reassuring manner.

The taxi continued its journey along Embankment, cutting up around Blackfriars and then up to Ludgate Circus and Holborn before depositing its passengers outside the court. Thankfully, there were no paparazzi.

Inside the building, I read the daily cause list. It was somewhat flattering to find myself allocated to the infamous Court Number 1. Outside court, lawyers had assembled, robed up with the usual copious bundles of files tied with red tape tucked under their arms.

Dunk had retained a leading silk, John Matthew QC, to defend him. Matthew had notched up a notable success in the Jeremy Thorpe conspiracy to murder case in 1979. He had appeared as defence counsel alongside George Carman QC, who had represented Thorpe. All defendants had been acquitted after a sensational trial that was hailed as the trial of the century.

As luck would have it, things were to turn out rather differently in the Dunk case.

"Good morning, James, I've got some bad news for you. There's been a slight change. Dunk is going to plead guilty," announced Manuell.

"What? I want to speak to him right now and find out what the hell's going on."

This was a dramatic turnaround even before the trial had started. The "gift" defence was reliant upon crucial evidence from witnesses from the Jordanian and Iraqi Embassies. However, mysteriously, all authority from the embassies for the witnesses to provide the evidence had been suddenly withdrawn without explanation.

When Dunk broke the devastating news to me, we were flabbergasted at the sudden and inexplicable turn of events.

"Listen, James, them soddin' Arabs have let me down and aren't coming to court so I'm absolutely fooked without them. Basil has advised us to plead guilty and they'll just fine us," said Dunk.

"You can't do that – you've got to fight this damn thing!" I insisted. "They're just out to bloody shaft you to put you out of business. Isn't it all to do with the FH70 artillery pieces you managed to sell to the Saudis?"

"Yes, I know that, son. They were always pissed off that I'd got that contract from under their noses with the help of Prince Mansour. But Basil says I'm stuffed without the witnesses, so what else is to be done?"

"Well I'm certainly not giving up when totally innocent. It's so unfair that you really have no option. What sort of justice is that?"

I thought that the whole situation was grossly unfair but, bereft of the witnesses, what could they do? It would have been difficult, if not impossible, for them to have maintained the defence without the witnesses. So reluctantly they pleaded guilty and, as a consequence, were ordered to pay some £20,000 in fines and costs. But Howroyd and I definitely weren't giving up without a fight.

With the main defendants out of the way, the whole affair was now utterly bewildering. I just couldn't believe what was happening. It was hoped that the gift defence would succeed and that would be the end of the matter. Furthermore, I was still wondering what had happened to the embassy witnesses and why I was still being prosecuted – and persecuted – now that Dunk and Schlesinger had reluctantly pleaded guilty. And to make matters worse, we'd lost our star witness, Major Keen, through illness.

It all seemed so bizarre – surely Customs had now got their man, so why pursue Howroyd and me any further? But Customs were determined to pursue us relentlessly, no matter what the consequences, in order to secure a conviction. Their stellar reputation was at stake.

Unknown to me at the time, this was to be a flagship "Arms-to-Iraq" prosecution and many others were to follow, including the infamous Matrix Churchill case. It was only then that I was to appreciate the true significance of my own case and the pressure Customs was under to secure a conviction no matter what. I was merely a pawn in the justice game, such as it may have been.

The trial judge was the Recorder of London, the late Sir James Miskin, known to the friendly and helpful court staff as "Whispering Jack". I had now become the main defendant and felt completely isolated without Dunk and Schlesinger. They were really the principal defendants in the case. One defence counsel remarked that it was "like playing Hamlet without the Prince of Denmark."

At court before the hearings, Howroyd and I appeared the epitome of respectability to the court staff. They regarded us as part of the defence team until it was pointed out that we were actually the defendants and, along with the judge, they treated us with the utmost courtesy.

There was some relief that we did not have to suffer the ignominy of having to spend time in the dock or the court cells. But we were still in the custody of the court for four weeks during a long and arduous trial – quite an ordeal for anyone, especially as it had been three years since Customs had raided Sterling.

Prosecuting counsel was less cordial. Customs has a fearsome prosecution reputation for protecting the Crown. They were well known for their determination to nail their man in order to maintain their reputation as a law enforcement agency and "*pour encourager les autres*" – hence the rationale for their draconian powers.

So Customs, with their unlimited resources, were able to retain one of the best criminal silks for the task, Anthony Arlidge QC, a formidable opponent assisted by junior counsel. David Howroyd and I, on the other hand, were not as fortunate and had to make do with only one counsel and were resolutely represented by a junior barrister, David Barnard, instead. This was hardly a level playing field. Co-defendants often have separate barristers because of a conflict of interest but in our case there was simply no need because our defence was similar and we were innocent of all charges. Anyway, a QC and separate counsel was simply a luxury we couldn't afford.

I found it hard to believe what was happening and the unfairness of it all. I kept on recalling the nineteenth-century Irish judge Sir James Mathew's well-known remark that, in England, justice is open to all, like the Ritz Hotel – so long as one can pay.

Mr Arlidge QC opened for the Crown in flamboyant style. He accused us of trying to "con" the authorities by using false destination certificates. Holding up to the jury and waving a Mark 5 Sterling silenced sub-machine gun at them, he claimed that "they were trying to send these to Iraq through the back door...."

Flabbergasted, I wondered why it was necessary to brandish a Sterling sub-machine gun in front of the jury and how that was likely to help them decide the case. My QC, Robin Auld, had previously warned me about this risk in 1983. It was crystal clear to me that I was being portrayed not as respectable businessman but as a "gunrunner" who was, therefore, guilty as charged.

I scrutinized the faces of the twelve jurors entranced by this obnoxious charade. Having gestured to my counsel, David Barnard, to intervene, he shook his head – the damage had already been done. It was extremely frustrating for me to have to just sit there powerless, watching this show trial knowing that the authorities had deserted me and were prepared to allow the conviction of innocent men.

Until now, their deadpan expressions betrayed no feeling for the case, save for one of boredom and one of resentment for having to spend four weeks of their precious time in an English court, so obviously completely alien to the majority of them. I had watched the fiasco of their being sworn in, with three or four managing to opt out and then having to be replaced.

Manuell and Barnard were cool, restrained and dismissive of the allegations of misleading the authorities. At all times they had been encouraging as the trial dragged on endlessly. I just had to sit there listening to the prosecution case waiting for my moment to present my side of things – the truth. I always felt that I would be acquitted and was surprised that the trial went on for so long.

It was also frustrating being tied up for so long in court away from the new business, BSA. There, the sixty-five employees were being put at risk because I simply could not initiate in time all the changes I had planned. Having had to hand back the day-to-day management, I really did not know what was going on in the daily routine up there, but clearly these changes were well overdue and had now been seriously delayed. The more the workings of the court limped on day by day, the more dire the situation up there would become. I was becoming desperate. It was an absolute nightmare and I felt very much out of control.

I was amazed at just how short was the working day of the court. A 10 o'clock start seemed so wasteful when I was used to one at 8 o'clock. A one and a half-hour lunch break usually spent at one of the tawdry local café/restaurants, followed by a short afternoon session, which was known to adjourn as early as 4 o'clock, seemed to my manufacturing mind not to be making the most of the overheads of these courts.

My mind wandered in and out of surrealism, through comedy, back to the abrupt terror of everyday life and my immediate future prospects.

Matters were not improved much by the prejudicial reporting of the trial in the local press. In 1983, I had been able to obtain an apology and retraction from the *Daily Express*, but now the law could not prevent the press reporting the daily proceedings of the trial. I was naturally concerned about any adverse effect on my personal reputation and, more particularly, the damage that this could cause to my new business.

There was further drama in the middle of the trial when a local newspaper, the *Romford Recorder*, printed a story that was incorrect and my lawyers had to write a letter to obtain a correction and an apology:

> We act for James Edmiston and for Mr David Howroyd.
> Our attention has been drawn to a news item headlined, "Export Attempt – 3 Accused 'Machine Gun Plot Foiled' – Court Told"….
> … the facts and allegations that you purport to give are incorrect, which is of particular concern since the jury have yet to consider their verdict….
>
> The following errors appear in your report:
> 1. 200 guns, not 2,000 guns were seized;
> 2. The guns were being exported by a company called Atlantic Commercial (UK) Limited, not our clients.
>
> We will be contacting you as soon as the trial is over to agree the wording of a suitable correction and apology….

This was an unwelcome distraction from the trial with the worry that the damage had been done and that there was little we could do until the end of the trial.

Eventually, it was my turn to give evidence. At last, I would now have an opportunity to put my case. There were various questions about the order and my response throughout was consistent: I was only the manufacturer; I had done business before with Jordan; Dunk had procured the order; and I had not misled the authorities.

Then came Howroyd's moment to give evidence. His was much the same as mine, and that he was only the works director. The local publicity had a bad effect on him and he was unfairly ostracized by his community and church.

After the conclusion of the defence case, David Barnard made a very powerful closing speech to the jury. The judge then summed up the case quite fairly and things seemed to be looking up for us. The judge then dismissed the jury to return a verdict. After four weeks of an interminable trial, I was faced with the final agony – waiting while the jury were out.

We sat together in court waiting for the jury to return. During any criminal trial, this is a time of great anxiety. The atmosphere was tense and we were both itching to learn the outcome. We had always enjoyed conviviality and informality and I tried to remain calm and in good humour.

After a short time the jury returned and filed back into the jury box with impassive expressions. The judge turned to the foreman and asked if the jury had reached a verdict. We sweated in anticipation and silence reigned. Suddenly, the foreman stood up and, looking towards the judge, announced a unanimous not guilty verdict for Howroyd – but there was no verdict for me.

There was a huge sense of relief for Howroyd. Everyone was very pleased that justice had finally been done. He was just an innocent bystander who should never have been prosecuted. But I now surmised that perhaps Howroyd had been prosecuted to bring pressure on me to plead guilty.

The relief over Howroyd's acquittal was short-lived. Now I became the sole focus of attention. Of course, I had expected to be acquitted together with Howroyd and just could not understand what had happened. Though I had never even entertained the thought of being found guilty, my thoughts now turned to the absence of a verdict and my own dilemma.

As the jury were unable to agree a unanimous verdict in my case, they were now sent away again to try to reach a majority decision. I was more than a little concerned about this strange turn of events and what could be the outcome.

Of course, the form of bowing, "M'ludding" ad nauseam, and the court niceties were quaint and amusing to start with, but when I wanted the whole matter moved on, it all began to pall, and I cursed the utter pomposity of it all.

"With respect, M'lud; my learned friend opposite might be confusing certain facts…." Being literally translated to everyday speak, this would come out slightly differently: "You bumbling old fart; can you not see that counsel opposite is mistaken, or has your narcolepsy kicked in again?"

As things turned out, I had to wait the whole day for the jury to return their verdict on me – it seemed endless. All this time, thoughts were flooding through my mind as I waited anxiously. While the jury was out and I was wondering what was really going on, to my surprise, one of the Customs investigators approached with a startling revelation that really shocked me: "Don't worry, son – we're not after you. We were only after Dunk."

"So you mean that you've put me through all this for nothing? That's outrageous," I protested.

The Customs man just shrugged his shoulders and said dispassionately, "Sorry, it's just the way we have to do things, isn't it mate? That's life."

This was hardly consolation for the destruction of a highly successful manufacturing business, my life and many other people's lives.

So, Customs had always been after Dunk. Howroyd and I had been prosecuted merely for the sake of expediency. Apparently, Sterling was the only British firm with which Dunk had done business but he had obviously upset the authorities, possibly over the FH70 contract to Saudi Arabia, and the order was out to get him. Customs were so determined to get Dunk, it seemed, that they were prepared to sacrifice Howroyd, the innocent works director, and me. But even so, it seemed odd that, following Dunk and Schlesinger's guilty pleas, the case was not dropped against us.

I felt completely confused and disappointed. I also felt angry – very angry indeed that Howroyd and I were merely scapegoats and a means to an end in a process that had kept me away from my new business and caused me many problems.

Eventually, the usher came back into court to say that the jury was now ready to return with the verdict. I sat behind John Manuell, alone, waiting for the result. It seemed an eternity. The jury then shuffled back into the jury box and sat down. The judge asked the foreman if the jury had reached a verdict. The old heart was fairly pounding away. The foreman responded: "No M'lud, we are unable to reach a unanimous verdict."

Silence fell over the court and I could barely understand what was going on or what was going to happen next.

"John, what's happening? Am I free?" I asked.

"Not exactly, James, we'll have to wait and see," he replied softly.

There followed a frantic exchange between counsel and there were some very tense and uncertain moments for me, which again seemed like an eternity. Events were now unfolding rapidly but I was still in the dark.

It was then the turn of David Barnard to address the court.

"M'lud, the jury has failed to reach a verdict in the case of my client, James Edmiston. This prosecution has not been made out. The defence now respectfully submit that it is not in the public interest for the Crown to pursue this case any further."

The judge looked towards me and counsel and reflected for a few moments on Barnard's submission. Prosecuting counsel was busy taking hurried instructions from the Customs corner.

The judge then turned towards Arlidge. "Mr Arlidge, in the light of the jury's decision and the defence submission, what is the Crown's position?"

"M'lud, the Crown offers no further evidence," replied Arlidge, with an air of resignation.

I still did not understand exactly what was happening and what this meant.

The judge then turned towards me: "Mr Edmiston, the Crown has decided not to offer any further evidence against you but I disallow costs. So I am now formally directing a verdict of not guilty to be entered on the record. You are now free to leave the court."

When I was acquitted, we shared no champagne outside the court. I felt no sense of triumph whatsoever. The verdict was not unequivocal; it was the Scottish equivalent of *not proven* and costs had been disallowed. I was drained and exhausted, bitterly disappointed and disillusioned at how the authorities could have let this happen to me. The main concern now became the survival of BSA and the welfare of my family.

Sisi had been present every day, sometimes sniffing for spicy variety around the other diverse cases being played out at the Bailey, but nevertheless was a pillar of support. Slingsby, always a true friend, when he heard the outcome, made a point of reiterating the belief he had always held in me. That was very warming and truly comforting. Paying his firm's bills was a further hurdle for the future that had yet even to cross my tiny mind.

Although acquitted, there was the stigma of prosecution and the media reports. I was almost nauseated with worry about the inordinate amount of damage inflicted on me, my family and the Sterling employees, totally unjustly.

The trial was over; I was a free man, unfettered to get on with my life, which should have been so much easier now. If only....

In order to escape from three years' hell, I managed to scrape some money together for a quick Christmas with my family and in-laws over in South Africa. As ever, it was a happy time; I was always desperately fond of my in-laws. Their home in the "Dark Continent" was always a haven, and the annual "Scramble for Africa" commencing at London Heathrow was, in spite of the normal aggro of seasonal air travel, well worthwhile.

I have so many friends that usually experience some form of combative state with their mothers-in-law as to be the norm. Never had I a cross word with mine, although some will argue that a 6,000-mile divide might have been a factor, if not an ideal.

Chapter 15

Euphoria?

In the course of time, I tried to reflect as to whom I could have made enemies of along the way.

Some two years before the Jordan affair, Major Keen, Howroyd and I had been entertained to lunch at the Dorchester by the then head of sales at the German rival firm of Heckler & Koch GmbH, one urbane and cultured Herr Jacquemard. In the course of lunch, I had been asked, "What price do you want for the cessation of Sterling production?" Unfortunately, out of blind pride, patriotism and loyalty to all at Sterling, I had refused to take the question seriously and dismissed it out of hand.

A short while later, some defence attachés in various British embassies and high commissions around the world contacted Sterling to investigate a circular from a section of the MOD. This requested that they push Heckler & Koch guns as they were now made at Enfield.

The guns were intended to be assembled at the RSAF Enfield. The injustice here was that Enfield was a Royal Ordnance Factory and part of the MOD. It was not a nationalized industry. Because of this, a "Preferred Source Policy" was operated whereby that facility had to be used and Sterling could not compete for any British Government requirement whatsoever for new small arms.

Sterling accepted this position. I had gone public with my utter disgust at RSAF Enfield hiding behind this policy and then going into a commercial partnership with a foreign rival company, selling foreign-made goods under their protective umbrella when a superior 100 per cent British product was available. Indeed, my point did create acute embarrassment.

A further and more serious subject was that of the standard service rifle. The government usually requires a new service rifle once in a fifty-year cycle. During this time the design and manufacturing expertise is lost to other more regularly demanded production engineering items. Here, the RSAF Enfield was called upon to produce a service rifle in 5.56mm calibre to be compatible with the American Army M-16 (Armalite AR-15) rifle.

Instead of trialling differently designed rifles, Enfield set about making their own. It was simply a knocked-off copy of the Armalite AR-18, which Sterling had been making under licence for Armalite Inc, the original designers of the AR-15 (M-16) and the AR-18. Enfield's only concession to originality was that their new rifle, the SA-80 (L85A1), was buttless, or "bull-pup", with the trigger well to the front of the chamber. All the early prototypes had Sterling-made essential parts.

Sterling was given no consultancy fee or any credit whatsoever for the design. Furthermore, Stanley Carroll, the director of Enfield at the time, got himself invited to Sterling, where he took notes of all the special-purpose machinery developed by David Howroyd in conjunction with Messrs Hodgson & Sanders of Crewe, a British machine tool manufacturer. He then ordered those same machines for Enfield. My thoughts on this conduct are not for publication.

Sterling had gained considerable experience in the manufacture of these types of rifles, as their first 5.56mm rifle had been licensed to Chartered Industries in Singapore, a government arsenal. The commercial attraction of collaboration with Armalite Inc had been a regular demand in the rifle's semi-automatic form from the American civilian market.

The downside was that Sterling was forbidden to improve the AR-18 by making it more robust for Squaddies. It would have created an administrative spares nightmare for Armalite, whose rifles had been made by them originally in California, then by Howa Machinery in Japan, and finally by Sterling.

In short, the AR-18 was not quite fit for use as a strong military rifle, and RSAF Enfield had copied it. In one or two very crucial but obscure areas, they had copied it wrongly. The result was probably the worst rifle that any major industrialized nation has ever foisted upon its armed forces in terms of balance, performance and reliability, quite apart from the initial exorbitant price that had been charged to the taxpayer.

I had gone public on exposing this fiasco. So had Jan Stevenson of *Handgunner* magazine. And he had been closed down.

Lord Trefgarne, a junior minister at the Defence Ministry, had written to me to say that I was wrong and that the rifle, after some initial teething problems, was now near perfect. The fact was that Mozambique, after a hugely destructive civil war, had been presented with a quantity of SA-80s by the British Government and had promptly rejected them for frontline use! That spoke volumes.

Later, the SA-80s were handed over to one of British Aerospace's more recent acquisitions, namely Messrs Heckler & Koch GmbH of Oberndorf, where the British taxpayer was charged a further sixty million Euros, or thereabouts, to modify all the guns so that they functioned properly. If Sterling had been consulted, the real problem lay in the bolt carrier assembly and the solution for that was comparatively simple.

The hard fact is that anybody connected with small arms procurement for the British Armed Forces in recent years should hide their head in shame. Exposure of that fact hardly endeared me or the former staff of Sterling to them. At what cost was it worth enforcing my silence?

Without my former empire, there was the question of how now to finance my struggle. The new owners of Sterling had undertaken to pay me a commission and consultancy should certain projected orders have been forthcoming. The orders came, but the whole consultancy dried up and, with too high an overhead, Sterling foundered in 1985, thereby causing even more litigation. The receivers, Casson Beckman, concluded that turnover at Sterling had declined after its sale in 1983 due to disputes between shareholders that led to that drop in turnover.

There was no question of me re-acquiring Sterling. This would have been entirely self-defeating in the light of the Customs prosecution. Sterling was eventually sold to Royal Ordnance in 1988, part of BAE Systems Plc.

The most agonizing factor of the whole trial for me was that having been stripped of one successful company, another, which was brimming with future opportunity, was slipping through my fingers while the trial proceeded at such a snail's pace. By the time I had been released from the Old Bailey and was back up to Birmingham, there were further problems afoot.

I was shattered, primarily by the experience of the trial, but also by the resultant display of misfortune and incompetence that had befallen BSA. The timing of the purchase was unfortunate given the subsequent unexpected commercial setbacks arising at the end of 1985. My absence at the trial in November was certainly a most unhelpful distraction.

I decided to call on the manager of Barclays Bank, Brian Williams – himself a gun enthusiast – and request that the bank appoint a receiver, as funds were becoming dangerously low. When I arrived back at the BSA office, the post had brought sufficient cheques to call the receivership off. I knew that there were sufficient assets to pay creditors, but I was so was utterly drained that the will to continue was spent.

Under the receivership, I immediately sold the hunting rifle part of the company to the Mohammad Dossul Company in Lahore, Pakistan, and the airgun side of the business to the Spanish airgun manufacturer, El Gamo.

What I was not prepared for were the exorbitant fees of the receivers, followed by the similarly exorbitant fees of the liquidators, as well as the outrageous delay of some four years to pay out the creditors, of which I was far and away the largest. The amounts collected by the receivers were further diluted by a host of spurious claimants that they, the receivers, were incapable of separating from those of the genuine.

The upshot was that the company was sold off in aggregate for nearly fifty per cent above what I had originally paid for it. Yet I was only able to collect just above 20p in the £1 after four years. It was a sad indictment of the professions and, in particular, it blew the absolute myth of "corporate recovery".

I was forced to sell my Argyll Road house to pay off the business mortgage used to buy BSA.

There was another debt of $100,000 owing to the First National Bank of Maryland taken out originally to start up Lanchester Inc in the USA. The debt and the company had been left out of the Sterling sale quite at variance with my intent. I had resolved to pay that off out of my proceeds of the BSA liquidation, which was, as I said, an inordinate time in coming.

In 1986 we purchased 14 Stanley Gardens W11. This was another saga and we had to sell it two years later.

We were unable to keep up the repayments on the mortgage and other debts were mounting up. In 1988, while trying to sell, the lender took us to court for possession and we ended up with a suspended possession order. I recall being extremely worried about this, as one would expect.

There was huge pressure on us to find a suitable buyer and to complete quickly. The agents were unaware of the possession order and it was vital to keep this confidential in order to achieve the best price possible in the circumstances. It was a very worrying time and a race against the clock. I kept wondering what would happen if the news leaked out somehow, and the potential consequences.

Fortunately, we were able to find a suitable buyer and complete in time, though we had to return to court to obtain a stay of execution. However, just when we thought all was well, I discovered that the bailiffs had changed the locks, had removed some of the purchaser's property and had left the property unsecured. As one can well imagine, the buyer was not too pleased and he sued us for return of the property and damages (more lawyers). Though it was eventually sorted out, it was a real hassle and so unnecessary. It looked bad and it was embarrassing having to explain what had happened. It was all very demeaning but frankly, there was little choice and we had to make the best of a very bad situation.

It was about a year after the trial ended that I learnt that Major Keen had died and I wrote to his widow, Barbara. If ever there was the personification of a company, it was Sterling in Major Keen. The over ninety-country customer list (including Jordan) is a fitting tribute on its own.

Chapter 16

New Adventures

In my early forties, I had to find myself some form of employment. For the first time in my life, I'd have to work for somebody else. I was not exactly relishing the prospect of this but what else could I do to support the family? A shooting friend, Geoffrey Bonas, was running a firm of headhunters (executive search consultants) that believed they controlled the majority shareholding in an aircraft manufacturer at Cardiff Airport called the Norman Aeroplane Company.

The founder, Desmond Norman, had been a co-founder of Britten-Norman on the Isle of Wight, which was the well-known manufacturer of the ubiquitous Islander and Trislander aircraft. This new enterprise had been started by Norman to make an elegant up-market crop duster called the Fieldmaster, which resembled a Spitfire. It had a proper undercarriage and a huge hopper, and was powered by a Pratt & Witney turbo-prop engine.

I was told that I was being headhunted to run the factory and to report to Norman at Rhoose Airport (Cardiff). I was greeted by Desmond Norman, who on hearing why I was there, told me in no uncertain phraseology to clear off, as he was still the majority shareholder and that he was intending to continue running the place.

"Hang on, Mr Norman, I can quite understand why you're piqued. I would be too, in your position. But as I'm down here, I'm genuinely interested in seeing round the factory."

"Oh, alright then."

Norman was proud of the factory, and the visit was most interesting. I made some suggestions to him and before I left he collared me.

"Look, you're not having my bloody job, but since you're down here, you're obviously not over busy yourself at the moment; would you work for me? I can't afford to pay much, but I guarantee you'll enjoy it, and we'll get you a pilot's licence."

Trying to restrain an outburst of enthusiasm, I smiled and said, "Of course; it would be a great privilege and pleasure to work for you. I'm very grateful, and accept your offer."

South Wales is an interesting area. I really enjoyed the six-month period working for Desmond Norman. My only regret is that I wasn't down there long enough to go with the lads in the factory to Cardiff Arms Park, as it was then known.

The job came to an end because the headhunting firm Wrightson Wood were on the cusp of a takeover by the employment giants, Blue Arrow. A few of the partners did not approve of the buy-out arrangements, and left to form their own company. So I was drafted in to become a headhunter in the fields of law and manufacturing – in reality, to make up numbers.

I was appointed to the board of Norman as a non-executive director but had to take the headhunting job as it paid twice what I was receiving from Norman and, at the time, my children's school fees were voracious.

There was nothing remarkable about my time at Wrightson Wood except that, coincidentally, I was on a professional assignment for Sheffield Forgemasters Ltd when news of the "Supergun" affair broke following the killing of Gerald Bull. The telephone kept ringing with enquiries as to what possible use the high precision forged oil pipes could be to the oil industry. The subject matter was a little too recent for me and I kept all my theories and opinions strictly to myself.

I helped Desmond Norman start an aircraft leasing company to rent out the five Fieldmasters that were engaged mainly in aerial fire-fighting, and introduced him to Andrew Mackinnon, whose grandfather had started car leasing in Australia and thus was prepared to introduce funds.

Norman Aeroplane ran out of funds, partially due to the fact that

Desmond Norman's excellent trainer, the Firecracker, was not adopted by the RAF. That honour went to the Tucano, which used the same engine, because it was probably part of an offset deal between British Aerospace and Brazil, where the Tucanos are built.

I managed to put together a rescue deal with Lloyds Bank in Salisbury to save Norman, but Mackinnon thought he could do a better deal by picking up the remnants in a receivership. Strictly speaking, he was right, but in practical terms, the new arrangements, with the assets of the company being placed with Optica as the CAA-approved builder, were a complete disaster. The professional advice given to Mackinnon by the accountants, as usual, was not the complete story. Norman lost his firm, and Mackinnon acquired a "pup".

As one grows older, job hunting becomes progressively harder. I saw a job advertised with a set of barristers' chambers, applied, and was taken on, on a temporary basis. The temporary job was highly entertaining and well remunerated, at least when the barristers were able to pay their clerks' fees. The tales are legion but irrelevant, except to say that I had studied law as an undergraduate, had been dragged into the law as a client many times, and now observed the workings of the law in action, first-hand.

Barristers' chambers are, if nothing else, action-packed, or, if you like, positively manic. It is a compelling setting for the legal drama of court cases played out against the backdrop of dynamic politics in chambers. Barristers are drawn from a complete cross-section of society. What formerly was an intellectual rich man's pursuit is now open to all, both to the intelligent and also perhaps to those who see the main attraction of the Bar as being more one of social status. Consequently, the Bar has exploded in numbers, and possibly the workload has not increased sufficiently to match this. The result has been that the quest for work has become more desperate, hence the jealous guarding of the sources of such.

All barristers should experience the cut and thrust of the criminal law in their early days at the Bar as it is an opportunity to gain court familiarity and the experience of being able to argue on one's feet.

Criminal law practice tends to originate with last-minute calls from police stations. The resultant briefs, if any, tend to be scant and ill-prepared. The high street solicitors, who by necessity form the bridge between client and barrister, have a huge problem making their practices pay, quite apart from trying to elicit fees from the Legal Aid Board.

Of course, the barristers will usually mouth off about the clerks for not having sorted out the problems before they begin. Such luxury is not always possible. They, the clerks, are also blamed for accepting the usually downward assessment of fees. Assessment is an attempt to bring some reality into the cost of administering justice, presumably for the benefit of the taxpayer in general.

The criminal law barristers' fees are dependent on the sometimes disorganized solicitors submitting all the fees appertaining to a case to the Legal Aid Board, whose administrative panjandrum trundles slowly forward. Obviously, differences arise as to the value of respective input to the case, and while lawyers in general tend to be more commercial, the average criminal barrister has had little or no experience of the sordid world of business.

Whenever I am asked to make a speech, I always allow one hour's preparation for every minute that I am on my feet. However relaxed I may seem, there is always the usual rush of adrenalin. So too with barristers; the continual prospect of the unpredictable accounts for stress and resultant strange behaviour patterns that manifest in many different and inexplicable ways that can, over time, accrue to a near madness.

Chambers certainly had its funny side. The inmates, tenants, barristers – call them what you will – tended toward lethality were they not gainfully occupied with plenty of work. They jealously tried to guard the source of their work (i.e. from their own instructing solicitors) from colleagues. If they were unavailable to take a case that had come in at short notice, only designated colleagues were "allowed" to stand in.

In extremis, when the clerk had to assign the work to another (available) tenant, then all hell would break loose when the original barrister found out, quite irrespective of being able to provide a proper service for the instructing solicitor and/or the lay client.

Quite apart from the colourful tenants, the conferences held in chambers between barristers, solicitors and lay clients produced visitors in chambers ranging from world-famous pop stars, businessmen and alleged illegal immigrants to some of a violent disposition and appearance, and even hookers. I unfailingly offered visitors non-alcoholic refreshments, and was one day rewarded for my efforts by one lady scantily attired in a miniskirt, showing me the full extent of what she did not wear beneath.

For all their faults and foibles, I did like them for their individuality. Time certainly flew by in the daily maelstrom. Seven whole years in a temporary post soon passed by, and this may have been a huge benefit in the light of other aspects of my tortured life.

Chapter 17

Cast Adrift

As the Berlin Wall came down in 1989, my marriage was suffering similar collapse through the strain of all the turmoil.

The stress, exhaustion and worry, together with the resultant effect on my life, family, and business, amounted to a living nightmare. Everything seemed to go wrong. I was not handling matters in the best way to end this run of trouble, though I did not know why. Absolute mental terror affected the physical side of my marriage. In short, from that time on, I just stopped enjoying life. From having been fairly outgoing, I now saw only a handful of close friends.

I lived in dread of being asked to social functions as I could not afford to reciprocate any hospitality. I did not go near a doctor or psychiatrist. The simple reason was that I would have felt guilty spending the money on myself. Life could not become any worse. Or could it?

I had resolved at all times to keep fit, and found solace in extreme exercise, mainly running (I had completed thirteen London marathons). It gave me time to think, but in so doing I was, of course, disregarding Horace Rumpole's pearl of wisdom that exercise is a shortcut to the cemetery.

At home, there were constant trivial interruptions, which seemed petty in the context of the trouble I was in. Consequently, I was irritable, ill-tempered and rude to my wife and family. It was, of course, not intended, but my fuse had become very short. Life with me had become unbearable.

The trial itself had also been an ordeal for us. Whilst confident of acquittal, I was still concerned about the risk. There were times when my wife would complain about lack of money and the family problems but I would just lose my temper and storm out of the house as it all became too much to cope with.

All of this also had a psychological effect on the children. Both the change in financial status and the gradual deterioration of the marriage must have been bewildering and unsettling, particularly for Harry, who was the youngest, being aged eight at the time.

My marriage and family life had always been easy, happy and fulfilling. There was a high level of friendship and intimacy. Sisi and I were very dependent on each other and were very much looking forward to enjoying our later years together with the children in comfort, good health, happiness and financial security. Instead, we found ourselves in a condition of great stress, accelerated and intensified by the deeply disturbing course of events. The whole affair had aged us both prematurely.

Eventually, without a proper income, we could not afford to keep up the family home in Argyll Road, and had to move again in 1987. The financial strain had simply become too much for us, especially the private school fees for the children. In effect, we used the equity in the various houses to fund most of our expenses, especially the school fees. We then had to move again in 1989 to a two-bedroom maisonette in W11, involving yet more disruption and distress.

So this now meant a further decline and that a family of six were living in two-bedroomed accommodation. Fortunately, my daughters were away at boarding school much of the time. But it was restricting (there was little privacy) and not what we had been used to at all in Phillimore Place.

Having loyally stood by me through some seven years of difficulty, things had become too much for my wife to bear, especially the financial burden. By 1990, the marriage had broken down irretrievably, and divorce was the only option. Sisi filed a divorce petition in November based upon my unreasonable behaviour. I left the family home at the end of that year and went to live with my mother at Montagu Mansions, London W1.

Sisi, relieved of horrific financial uncertainty, went to live with her young South African inamorato in his prestigious country house in Warwickshire, although she and I remained friends at all times.

I tasted bachelor freedom, but it was tinged with penury, since I was always faced with the responsibility of maintaining and educating four children who had suffered from the upheavals. I was determined to provide the best education possible even if that meant poverty for me and living like a church mouse in my mother's rented flat. God bless my dear mother.

Unable to afford private education in central London, I had chosen the more economic option of boarding school. But quite apart from all the laudable intentions and the indispensable bursaries, discounts and loans from friends, the sad reality was that I was always in a chronic state of debt. It was during this difficult time, in 1991, that I took that temporary job as practice manager of a set of barristers' chambers at 3 Temple Gardens that was to last for seven years, as described in the previous chapter.

The income from chambers was purely on a commission basis as a percentage of the fees received by the respective barristers. However, for at least two months I received not a penny, since my commission was deemed to start from work that I had actually "clerked". The barristers were all different, individual, and ranged from being highly entertaining to being crashing bores.

As the chambers grew in size, my pay grew proportionately. But many barristers struggle to manage cash flow and are not always the quickest of payers. There was always skirmishing in chambers, and some of the newer tenants objected to the clerks' earnings being well in excess of theirs (quite a common feature at the Bar). This was a problem that was to bring some unpleasantness later on.

When 'clerking' at chambers, I had been introduced to a particularly good-looking lady graduate of the LSE (London School of Economics) who was keen to read for the Bar and qualify as a barrister. We had much in common and struck up quite a friendship. One Sunday, I was commanded by Sisi to come to Sunday lunch at the house in Warwickshire as the whole family would be there. I had a previous engagement with Tess, but decided to compromise since the insistence to appear was so strong. I duly took Tess with me and immediately chalked up huge "street cred" with my kids for my choice of companion. Outcomes are often hard to forecast.

So all was not gloom, and there was a new bright star in my life. I was introduced to Sally on New Year's Eve 1991 at some mutual friends' quiet party. Sally had had her own marital difficulties in the past, but had the care and responsibility of her three children. That apart, she was now released. Smiling, pretty, blonde, petite and well-travelled, there was an instant attraction.

Our relationship grew. Sally's origins were in Wales, a fact that I managed to overlook by suppressing my inborn prejudices. She had been brought up in Lancashire. Successive boarding schools had been followed by music and modelling, and before marrying at an early age she had enjoyed living, incredibly, in Birmingham.

She had married a German and, after living in Hamburg for a year, where her German became fluent, she went to live in Jakarta. I vaguely remembered staying in the Hotel Indonesia when travelling there with David Howroyd and, while breakfasting in the coffee shop of that hotel, talking to a young English lady whose little daughter was dressed in blue. Certainly, Sally had been living there at the time, waiting until her home was ready for occupation.

Sally was incredibly supportive and on more than one occasion helped out with liquidity difficulties over school fees when these had fallen behind and the bursars were unwilling to allow the children to start the term on promises of jam tomorrow. "Mr Edmiston, I'm afraid we're running a business here," was the general response to a request for yet further extended credit.

I bit my tongue at the suggestion that they were businesses, whereas, in reality, their survival depended on being allowed charitable status for taxation purposes. I would have loved to have reminded them of this but thought it prudent to keep my mouth firmly shut.

It was during 1991 that I decided to write a book, *The Sterling Years*, which was published in 1992 (it was republished in 2011). It had been a cathartic exercise to set the record straight. The book was dedicated to the staff and workforce, as well as the customers of

Sterling. I suppose that I had always thought about writing something about the history of Sterling and the exceptional loyalty that the employees had shown to me.

I had some spare time, and perhaps the divorce had something to do with timing. I had now lost everything: my business, my home, and my marriage. It was to some extent an attempt to reflect on the past success of Sterling, what had been its future potential, and all that had been lost. It was not intended to be a political book or to embarrass the government.

Written quickly from memory with a few notes, it was never meant to be a best-seller or a huge financial success; indeed, the initial royalties were only some £1,000, but that meant a lot to me in those dark days when I had to scrape together every last penny in order to pay school fees and just exist.

Chapter 18

Great Scott!

*Truth is so precious that she must be attended
by a bodyguard of lies.*
Winston Churchill

In 1992, while I was settling in at chambers, the nation was gripped by the sensational Old Bailey trial of the three Matrix Churchill directors, Paul Henderson, Peter Allen and Trevor Abraham, who were charged with alleged illegal export to Iraq of machine tools for munitions. Henderson was represented by an impressive defence team headed up by Geoffrey Robertson QC and Kevin Robinson of Irwin Mitchell, solicitors.

The stakes were high for Customs after the Supergun fiasco. Sir Brian Unwin, the Chairman of Customs & Excise, had expressed concerns that the Matrix Churchill case did not turn into a repeat of the Supergun case. Customs had to drop the charges in that case on the advice of Attorney General Patrick Mayhew that the prosecution would probably fail. So Customs could not afford to suffer another embarrassment like this.

Sir Brian was adamant:

> To put it crudely I don't want a repeat of the Gun affair....
> Apart from the damaging effect on morale, we don't have the
> resources to waste on complex cases that are unlikely to lead to
> a successful prosecution.

Customs investigators were furious that the Supergun case had been dropped and felt betrayed by government departments. That Christmas, they made up a spoof Christmas card addressed to

Customs investigators from HMG, the DTI, the MOD, and the Attorney General, showing a body face down on the ground with a dagger in its back.

Customs was determined to proceed with the Matrix Churchill prosecution no matter, whatever the consequences. Thinking back to my case, was this history repeating itself?

During the trial, Paul Henderson, the managing director, had revealed details of his work for the security services and of providing intelligence on Iraqi military procurement. This had helped the allies in Operation Desert Storm.

The directors' defence was clear-cut: the government knew about and had encouraged the export of machine tools for making munitions to Iraq. The Howe Guidelines in 1985 restricting arms exports to Iraq and Iran had been relaxed secretly. The Department of Trade and Industry minister, the late Alan Clarke, had encouraged manufacturers to emphasize "general military use" on licence applications to the DTI. And anyway, the government was quite aware of the situation from Henderson's intelligence reports on Iraq.

During the Matrix Churchill trial, members of the security services gave evidence supporting Henderson's account of his intelligence gathering and described him as "a very brave man". Though Customs was not best pleased and complained to the security services, the response was unequivocal: Henderson had provided valuable information and was, indeed, courageous. The Iraqi execution of *Guardian* journalist Fazad Bazoft in March 1990 for alleged spying was proof enough.

The case soon collapsed at the close of the prosecution case after Robertson's devastating cross-examination of Alan Clarke. Secret documents were disclosed showing that Henderson had been helping the intelligence services and the government was fully aware of the exports. The trial had ended spectacularly, in November 1992, when Alan Clarke accepted what had happened and that the government had been economical with the "*actualité*" – HMG had known all along what was happening with defence exports to Iraq.

So the Crown had to drop the charges. It was a humiliating and embarrassing spectacle for the government, especially the misuse of

Public Interest Immunity Certificates to hide the truth of its knowledge and complicity. The Matrix Churchill directors were publicly vindicated. They celebrated outside the Old Bailey with champagne surrounded by hundreds of paparazzi desperately scrambling for interviews and photographs that would be beamed around the world. There had been no such public vindication for me and little consolation for the 600 Matrix Churchill employees who had lost their jobs.

Though Sterling had never traded with Iraq, I was struck by the similarities of the two prosecutions concerning government knowledge and encouragement of exporters. HMG had also turned a blind eye in my case to the fact that goods sent to Jordan could end up in Iraq.

So, in both cases, the directors should never have been prosecuted.

Before the Iraq/Iran War, HMG had supplied arms and training to Saddam's government, especially in artillery, and hence setting up munitions production in Iraq. It was good business for the UK and good for jobs. The Treasury was also in an exposed position as guarantor to British exporters for many millions of pounds under the Export Credits Guarantee Scheme.

I had known years before that Matrix Churchill was Iraqi-owned. It was making superb machine tools, many of which were developed for ordnance production. To say that our government did not know these facts would be arrant nonsense. As things stand today, perhaps we made a real mistake in Iraq. One can be so wise with hindsight.

Paul Henderson and Peter Allen, another Matrix Churchill director, had actually spent a night in custody before being released on bail because of a technicality. This was later to become a vital factor for them, as well as for myself, in the long battle for compensation.

In the wake of the collapse of the trial, many senior figures in law and politics thought it was a disgrace that the government was prepared to let innocent men go to jail in order to spare it the embarrassment about government knowledge and the fact that it had actually helped to arm Saddam Hussein before his invasion of Kuwait in August 1990. There was also huge widespread public concern, and many senior judges were extremely concerned about the public's loss of faith in the court system.

In response to this, John Major immediately announced the setting up of the Scott Inquiry to look into the Matrix Churchill prosecution along with several other cases, including ours. He gave Lord Justice Scott enormous scope in the terms of reference:

> Having examined the facts in relation to the export from the United Kingdom of defence equipment and dual-use goods to Iraq between 1984 and August 1990, and the decisions reached on the export licence applications for such goods and the basis for them, to report on whether the relevant departments, agencies, and responsible ministers operated in accordance with the policies of Her Majesty's Government; to examine and report on decisions taken by the prosecuting authority and by those signing Public Immunity Certificates in R v Henderson and any other similar cases that he considers relevant to the issues of the inquiry; and to make recommendations.... All ministers who are called will give evidence; all civil servants who are called will be instructed to co-operate; all papers that the inquiry calls for will be made available....

This must have rung alarm bells all around government that it would open a huge can of worms and heads would roll. Armies of civil servants would be enlisted to protect the state, ministers and themselves.

Although this sent shivers across Whitehall, its significance had not been apparent to me at the time and neither had the fact that Scott would also be looking into our case. I had not really been following events closely in the course of various witnesses giving their evidence to the inquiry.

Matrix Churchill was discussed in chambers, but I hadn't paid too much attention to that case since I was always running around chambers like a blue-arsed fly. It was then that one of the tenants in chambers, like a baby cuckoo, piped up, "Why the hell don't you get us prestigious cases like that?"

At a loss for words, my only reply was that a possible reason was that we did not field Geoffrey Robertson QC or his ilk in chambers.

However, I took the question to heart, and wondered how I could get around the Dickensian rule that barristers and their clerks must not tout for business. So I hastily arranged a Christmas cocktail party by way of an innocent seasonal celebration. Apart from selecting the wine and nibbles, I recruited a spellbinding string quartet of delectable ladies from the Guildhall School of Music. On the appointed evening, chambers filled with prospective instructing solicitors from all kinds of law firms. I had invited a former rugby-playing friend, Tim Archer, who was the senior partner at Richards Butler, a highly respected City firm.

I was showing Archer around chambers and, seeing one of the room doors closed, took him in while announcing that one of our star performers worked from his desk in there. No sooner had I switched on the light than I saw the gentleman in question flat out on the floor snoring like a sleeping sow. Before I could beat a hasty retreat, Archer had viewed this divine revelation, and thought it a huge joke. I was hardly surprised that Richards Butler did not inundate us with work.

However, although I did not know it at the time, the Matrix Churchill case did have a significant indirect consequence for me. A former member of the Customs Investigations Department had advised a young solicitor to brush up his knowledge of malicious prosecution and the Home Office compensation scheme, and then referred Peter Allen of Matrix Churchill to him. That solicitor was one Lawrence Kormornick and the referral was to change the course of our lives.

But the irrepressible Reg Dunk *had* been following the news, very closely, in the hope that something new would emerge about the Arms-to-Iraq cases, and our case in particular. He was wondering whether it could throw new light on what had caused the sudden disappearance of the key witnesses, which had led him to change his plea to guilty. Dunk had not enjoyed the best of times after conviction. The resultant fines and bad publicity had led to the demise of his business and he suffered hard times in his later years.

By coincidence, about eighteen months after starting at chambers, I was at the Royal Courts of Justice seeing a listing officer, when I received a telephone call from Reg Dunk. He had heard a rumour in June 1993 that the Scott Inquiry was about to hear some important revelations about our case.

"Reg! How the hell are you? What's new?"

"Well, Roger and I don't talk anymore, which is sad, and business isn't good at all, but at least the wife and I are well. So how's life treating you, James?"

"I'm afraid all this broke up my marriage. Too many worries and my poor wife buggered off with some South African bloke who appears to have a crock of gold. Mind you, I can't say I blame her."

"I'm sorry, James, it's been really rotten for you. But listen up – I've some interesting news for you."

"What's that?"

"Well, have you been following this Scott Inquiry thing about arms going to Iraq?"

"Can't say I've had time, working in this madhouse."

"Well, I think you should go and listen in. Seems the bastards may have actually fixed our witnesses."

"What are you talking about? Are you serious? That's absolutely appalling!"

"James, I've just heard that some Foreign Office bloke is giving evidence today about our case to Inquiry…. Could you go down there to listen in? Might be bloody important for us, you know. Always wondered what actually happened to them witnesses and why they fooked off."

Dunk sounded elated but I had rather mixed feelings about the news. Having tried to put the devastating effects of the last ten years behind me and just concentrate on rebuilding my life, I wasn't sure if I really wanted to rake over the past.

Certainly, whenever I reflected on what had happened, I felt sad recalling all that I had lost in my personal and business life. But at the same time it was important to get to the bottom of things and it was so odd that the witnesses had just disappeared.

"Okay, I'll do what I can and let's speak later," I told Dunk.

"Can you make next Wednesday for lunch at Simpsons?" he asked.

"Nothing whatever would stop me from being there. I really look forward to seeing you again."

"Likewise."

Just to be facetious, I added, "And how's your beak-nosed friend Khalid the Corruptible, whom I've never met?"

"Haven't seen him for years. I think he went home. He was a Jordanian, you know."

I was stunned and reflected on what Dunk had said and wondered why Customs had made such a fuss if Khalid was, in fact, a Jordanian.

Chapter 19

Bad Show

I strode through the swinging doors of the Royal Courts of Justice to the usual bevy of protestors and photographers. Fortunately, I was seen immediately by the Clerk of the Lists, and finished the business with him within five minutes – it could have taken two hours or more.

There was some time to spare from chambers. I rushed over the zebra crossing outside of the RCJ, as it is known in the profession, with my mind completely focused on getting to the inquiry as quickly as possible so as not to miss any revelations about the Dunk case and what had happened to the witnesses.

A car that had stopped for another pedestrian at the crossing moved off, completely oblivious of me. I saw what was happening in time and jumped onto the bonnet. The car suddenly lurched to a stop again and I was thrown off onto the road. I was slightly shaken but otherwise unhurt. The driver was quite shocked, very contrite, and apologized profusely.

"That's alright; you obviously didn't see me. Please don't worry; I'm not hurt," I reassured him. Running around Regent's Park every day of my life had had some benefit, it seemed. The driver moved off slowly and before I had reached Middle Temple Lane, four or five men rushed up to me from all points of the compass.

"I say. I saw that. I've got his number. Are you quite sure you're alright? Absolutely sure? Well, if it gets at all painful, here's my card. Where there's blame, there's a claim and you have nothing to lose – it's all no win, no fee, so it won't cost you a penny." I was festooned with visiting cards, all denoting that, without exception, the apparently concerned citizens were all members of the legal profession.

"I'm really okay, but thanks all the same," I chuckled, heading off across the Temple and towards Embankment to hail a cab. Then, under my breath, I expectorated that oft-quoted cliché, "Bloody ambulance-chasers!"

I soon arrived at 1 Palace Gate, where the inquiry was being held. The inquiry was a political landmark that had already thrown light on Whitehall's shadowy world of secrecy, half-truths and even outright lies. Senior politicians had appeared at the inquiry, including John Major, Michael Heseltine, Alan Clark and Margaret Thatcher.

I slipped into the room where Lord Justice Scott was presiding. A pleasant-looking man who was a South African, Scott had been well educated at Michaelhouse in Natal, and had been at Cambridge, where the detribalization process had obviously taken root. In true South African tradition, Scott had been no mean sportsman, taking a rugby blue, and he was frequently pictured in the newspapers cycling to the inquiry. Scott was widely known to be robust and independent and famous as the judge who had dismissed the government's attempt to ban the publication of *Spycatcher*, the memoirs of the former MI5 agent Peter Wright.

Looking around the room, there were some slightly familiar faces. I could not immediately work out whether they were just court officials whom I had met in my role as a barrister's clerk or from a former walk of life. Beside Scott sat Counsel to the Inquiry, Presiley Lamorna Baxendale QC.

According to *The Independent*, Baxendale had been educated at St Mary's Wantage, at Westminster and St Anne's College Oxford, all funded from the fruits of her father's Turkish delight business. Before the Scott Inquiry, she was known mainly for her name (parents often have the habit of inflicting unfortunate names on their offspring). Baxendale was now acquiring a fearsome reputation as the government's chief tormentor and her victims had included William Waldegrave, Minister of State at the Foreign Office, who conceded that approving exports to Iraq had turned out to be "a wrong judgment", and Ian McDonald, head of Defence Export Services

Secretariat at the Ministry of Defence, who, when asked about how parliamentary questions should be answered, had famously replied: "truth is a difficult concept."

I began to concentrate. An elderly man was sitting at the table opposite Scott, who was listening intently to his every word. It appeared that Sir Stephen Egerton had been our man somewhere in the Middle East at the time of the Jordanian order.

Stephen Loftus Egerton, born in India, was a career civil servant who came from a long tradition of public service. From Eton, he went up to Trinity College Cambridge to read classics and had entered the Civil Service in 1956, becoming an expert in Middle-Eastern affairs and an ambassador to Saudi Arabia. At the time of the Dunk order in 1982, he had been Under-Secretary for the Middle East.

Having settled down, I suddenly became aware of what was being discussed. I wondered how Scott and Baxendale would question Egerton, the classics scholar and senior career diplomat. Perhaps they would treat this as some sort of classics seminar, in which Egerton, with some gentle prompting, would interpret the British Government's Middle-East arms export policy and explain what had happened in the Dunk case. In this way a dialogue could be built on mutual respect in order to avoid confrontation with Egerton becoming defensive and evasive.

Scott began by politely welcoming Egerton to the inquiry as if inviting him in for a cosy fireside chat.

"Thank you very much for coming here to help us ..." said Sir Richard.

By expressing his appreciation, Scott was hoping to send a message that there was nothing personal against Egerton. But his soft tone belied the fact that this would be a probing investigation into government arms export policy during the Iran-Iraq War from 1980 to 1985, the Dunk case, and the mysterious disappearance of the embassy witnesses.

"Very glad to be here, Sir Richard, and I will help all I can, but I must warn you that my memory is rather weak after the lapse of time," replied Egerton apologetically.

I was not expecting such an enthusiastic response and wondered just how glad Egerton would be feeling by the end of the day. I tried to hide the wry smile on my face. Egerton had not hesitated to mention straightaway a "weak memory" – a convenient way to cover up any government embarrassment, I thought.

My mind began to wander back over events in the Matrix Churchill case where so-called gagging orders had been used to avoid government embarrassment. So, would Egerton also escape by relying on memory loss to protect his masters?

The questioning began slowly but purposefully with the background to Foreign Office arms export policy before the introduction of the Howe Guidelines in 1985 and the tightening of arms export to the Middle East. Egerton explained that he had been the Under-Secretary for the Middle East Desk (MED) from 1982 to 1986. He had held a senior position at the time of the Dunk order in 1982, so I was hoping that he *would* be able to shed some light on the sudden and inexplicable disappearance of the key embassy witnesses.

After the initial questioning, Scott was keen to move on quickly to get to the heart of UK arms export policy with Iraq. Egerton was surprisingly frank about this.

"The whole essence, the *raison d'être* of MOD Sales was to push sales ..." Egerton told Scott, unequivocally.

Pushing arms sales to Iraq was well known to many within and outside government. In the early 1990s, I was very familiar with the extensive efforts of the MOD and the DTI "to push sales" to Iraq and other Middle Eastern countries. Government encouragement and knowledge of exports to Iraq had been the main feature also in the spectacular collapse of the Matrix Churchill trial in November 1992, after the judge had ordered disclosure of secret documents. Disclosure had also revealed that the aim of government policy from 1980 had been "a great sales push" in arms exports to the Middle East by the MOD and DTI.

What an ironic coincidence, I reflected. Customs had seized the Jordanian order at the same time that the MOD was hosting a sales exhibition in Jordan in order to "push sales" to the Middle East.

The questioning then moved swiftly on to the core of UK foreign policy in Iraq and Iran. Egerton again was unequivocal.

"They [the UK] were extremely keen that Iraq should not be defeated and they wanted to make good profits in the process," he explained.

Another frank admission, thought I. He was also aware that numerous Tory ministers had visited and courted Iraq over this period and thought that it was a wonderful trading opportunity. These ministers were unconcerned that Iraq was a dictatorship and that the dictator, Saddam Hussein, had an agenda to destroy his neighbours.

Putting it crudely, it was clear from Egerton's answers that the UK thought it was no bad thing if Arabs killed each other and even better if the UK could also profit from it – hardly an ethical foreign policy. And, in order to cover up the policy, the UK was also indifferent to the prosecution, conviction and imprisonment of innocent British businessmen who had helped the UK to profit from this trade, I surmised.

The questioning was now gathering pace and moving on to the important issue of Foreign Office knowledge of where goods were actually ending up in the Middle East. I was intrigued to discover that the Foreign Office had become aware in the early 1980s that Jordan was a conduit for Iraq.

When asked about this, Egerton said that he had entertained suspicions about this before 1984 that deepened after the Dunk case. I wondered if the Foreign Office and other government departments were also aware of this prior to 1984. If so, why had the authorities allowed the Sterling order to proceed and then prosecuted me and the others? But curiously, the terms of reference of the inquiry had been limited to the period *after* 1984.

Just as things were beginning to get really interesting, the inquiry adjourned for lunch, so I would have to wait until the afternoon session to hear the revelations about my case.

I reflected on the morning session. Egerton had admitted that UK policy was to export goods to the Middle East and to profit from the

Iran-Iraq War and that the government was aware in the early 1980s that Jordan was being used as a conduit for Iraq. The scene was now set for the heart of the questioning about the investigation into the Dunk case and what had in fact happened to the embassy witnesses.

The afternoon session began with Baxendale completing her investigation into Foreign Office knowledge of Jordan as a conduit for Iraq. Unsurprisingly, Egerton was not terribly helpful about what he personally knew at the time. Though reports about the use of Jordanian facilities had been sent to the Foreign Office, Egerton was unable to say whether he had seen them himself because he had been "travelling".

So after a great deal of probing about the use of Jordan as a diversionary destination before 1983, the focus of the inquiry then turned to the Dunk case.

"What I would now like to do is to ask you a bit about Major Dunk," Baxendale said in a seemingly disarming manner in order to put Egerton at ease.

Now I listened intently, completely unaware of the murky story and series of revelations that were about to emerge – revelations that would change the course of the rest of my life. The old heart began to pound as Baxendale asked Egerton to look at an important Customs document.

"Could you go to FCO 112, Part 2, page 27; this is a Customs and Excise document, I believe," Baxendale asked politely. She seemed keen to question Egerton about a letter sent from Customs to the Foreign Office; FCO 112, Part 2, page 27 would become a key document in the Scott Inquiry and in my long battle for justice.

Baxendale began by explaining to Egerton that this was a letter dated 25 February 1983 (one week after the Sterling raid) from Mr Knox, Chief Investigation Officer at Customs, sent to Patrick Wogan at the Foreign Office. The letter attached reports concerning two Customs visits to the Iraqi Embassy to discuss the Dunk case and the gift defence.

"Page 27, 23 February 1983; it refers to a visit made on 18 February by Mr Conway to the Iraqi Embassy, to make inquiries in connection with a shipment of arms detained at the Victoria Deep Wharf," Baxendale continued.

She then read out slowly to Egerton the contents of a Customs report about what the Iraqi Ambassador had said and Customs' concern about the embassy witnesses giving evidence:

> With regard to the exportation of the 200 Sterling sub-machine guns: The ambassador stated that it was a typical example of the generosity between Arab countries....
>
> My only concern is the possible effect this story may have in future criminal proceedings.... It may be prudent for us to confront the ambassadors with the contradictory evidence in our possession before such an eventuality becomes fact in the hope that this will deter them from taking a potentially embarrassing course of action.

I was shocked and just couldn't believe what I'd just heard. The letter to the Foreign Office had revealed that Mr Conway, a Customs chief investigation officer, had visited the Iraqi Embassy on 18 February 1983, the day of the raid, after the visit to Sterling's factory. This was to interview the ambassador about the Dunk case but he was not then available for interview.

But then, on 21 February, just three days after the raid, two Customs investigation officers, Mr Conway and Mr Byrne, had revisited the embassy and interviewed the ambassador. The ambassador had confirmed the gift defence and that Dunk was unaware of the true destination of the goods.

I leaned forward eager to hear Egerton's response to Customs' plan that the embassy witnesses should not give evidence. Though I had expected some expression of regret from this senior diplomat for the misconduct, the response was quite different.

"I must say, I do congratulate Customs and Excise in smoking out those two embassies as they did," insisted Egerton.

I'd always thought that Foreign Office officials were decent chaps who played it with a straight bat. So it was shocking to discover that the officials had, in fact, conspired to stop the embassy witnesses from appearing at the trial and furthermore, that Egerton even considered congratulations to be in order.

Raised eyebrows betrayed the fact that Scott and Baxendale were not greatly impressed with either the misconduct or Egerton's indifference. Baxendale now decided that this was the moment to suggest this was not cricket.

"What they are hoping to deter them from doing is appearing and giving evidence…. That is not, in the British way of conducting criminal cases, a good thing for Customs to be attempting to achieve, is it?" she asked in a damning way.

But before Egerton had chance to reply to such a serious accusation, Scott quickly intervened to moderate the language in order to avoid Egerton becoming defensive at this early stage.

"It reads like a decision to try to avoid having these embassy staff members appear in court to tell what the author plainly thinks will be revealed as a cock and bull story," suggested Scott.

"Yes," replied Egerton, grateful for the intercession and hoping that a short, affirmative response might bring some closure to this painful exchange and avoid any further embarrassment.

As I tried to grasp the reality of the situation, I pondered as to why the officials had tried to stop the witnesses from appearing at trial. Was this the usual process in a criminal case, and if not, why so in this case? If Customs had a strong case, then why block the witnesses? I was not usually a conspiracy theorist but was now beginning to become very suspicious and concerned about the officials' behaviour.

I reflected on Baxendale's principle of the right to a fair trial. She was absolutely correct that the officials' behaviour was not "the British way of conducting criminal cases."

It was becoming crystal clear to me that officials had conspired to prevent the exercise of the right of every Englishman to a fair trial. This seemed even worse misconduct than in the Matrix Churchill case, or any of the other associated prosecutions. It struck to the core of conscience, offending all the notions of fair play.

I now began to feel quite dizzy and flushed. My heart raced at the thought of how unfair this was, and all sorts of questions flooded into my mind. The defence was a matter for the jury to decide at the trial, wasn't it? Surely, the officials should not have tried to stop the witnesses attending trial? Wasn't this a conspiracy to pervert the course of justice? How else could this be interpreted?

Customs were well known for their determination to nail their man no matter what, but members of the Foreign Office were supposed to be gentlemen who would certainly not lend themselves to this sort of conduct.

There was so much more to think about but I focused my attention back on the questioning. Scott's intervention to reassure Egerton had only served to make Baxendale even more inquisitive about the officials' subsequent behaviour in 1985.

There had been an unexplained two-year gap in the record after the embassy visits in February 1983. Neither I nor my lawyers had ever been able to understand the two-year delay in proceeding to trial. Now Baxendale was also keen to investigate this interval and the continuation of the plot in 1985.

"Shall we go on with what happens in 1985?" she suggested softly, inviting Egerton to interpret what happened next.

Baxendale then referred Egerton to a telephone call between Customs and Foreign Office officials:

"HM Customs and Excise had held a pre-trial review on 30 September. The defence said that the accused would all be pleading not guilty and would be calling members of the embassy staff from both embassies as witnesses for the defence.... It was Mr Cassey's view that the interests of the embassies would not be served by members of the embassies' staff agreeing to appear for the defence."

Egerton now sensed that it would be inadvisable not to distance himself and his masters from such inappropriate behaviour. Congratulations were certainly no longer in order.

"A most extraordinary opinion, is it not? I would have called them and got them to remove their immunity from themselves," replied Egerton.

Baxendale was heartened by this response and wanted to probe further into the plot. She could sense that Egerton's resolve was weakening and she was now seeking some affirmative responses.

"But is it not right that, generally, you would not expect it to be left to a jury to decide whether or not to accept a story as ludicrous or not?" asked Baxendale.

"I would, yes," replied Egerton.

Baxendale now saw her chance to nail the point.

"And you would not expect someone from Customs and Excise or someone from the Foreign Office to decide to try to obviate that embarrassment by stopping the witnesses from appearing?"

I was really keen to hear the answer to the accusation, and the phrase "stopping the witnesses from appearing" positively resonated in my mind. Scott did not intervene. But Egerton would be pushed no further with this language and was not prepared to answer such a direct question. So he gave an evasive response.

"If the ambassador agreed, of course; he would have to agree to that and, in both these cases, they would rather have died, I think, than agree."

Baxendale thought it best to now change tack slightly and direct Egerton's attention to what happened next, and then to rephrase the question about interference with the defence witnesses. So she told Egerton that a note of the telephone call had been sent to a Mr Pigott, who annotated it with a manuscript note addressed to Mr Nixon, the head of NENAD (North East and North Africa Department). The note began:

MED are contemplating having an informal word with the Iraqi Ambassador to point out the possible pitfalls of waiving immunity.

"Yes," replied Egerton, looking anxious about what was coming next.

Baxendale then read out a manuscript note from another Foreign Office official, Mr Harding:

I have passed on the thought at X to the Iraqi Embassy, and have told Mr Cassey of our action. Both the ambassador and the First Secretary who gave information to the police in 1983 are now gone – so there is no chance of the embassy helping.

"Yes," replied Egerton, keen to move on and looking for an escape route from the trap being set.

Baxendale then read an internal Foreign Office note sent from Mr Pigott to Mr Nixon:

> MED have had an informal word with the Iraqi Ambassador to say (a) this is none of the Foreign Office's business, but (b) it would perhaps be best if the ambassador did not agree to waive immunity. I am not sure that we need to make the same noises to the Jordanians.... But if you think it appropriate I could have a word with counsellor Kadi.

Baxendale was keen to reach the climax of the questioning without any interruptions and this time, Scott merely observed in silence. Before Egerton had any chance to intervene, Baxendale revealed the most damning piece of evidence of the whole inquiry, which would haunt the authorities forever. Slowly, she read to Egerton Nixon's incriminating response to Pigott:

> I confess to innocent reluctance to connive at impeding the course of justice! But you might gently enquire when talking to Kadi on other business.

Baxendale then read Mr Pigott's response to Egerton:

> Spoke to Mr Kadi, who was grateful and agreed with C and E's advice.

Silence reigned. Baxendale had chosen this moment carefully. She could see that Egerton was visibly unsettled by these revelations and felt victory was in sight. This time there would be no escape for him. After a short pause to allow Egerton to comprehend the full gravity of the situation, Baxendale looked him directly in the eye and asked gently, "Looking at those last comments about conniving and impeding the course of justice, those are correct, are they not?"

"Yes, I am afraid so, yes they are," replied an exhausted Egerton, looking down at the papers to hide his shame and embarrassment, clearly praying for the agony to end and wondering why it had fallen to him to be in this invidious position. He had wanted to please his masters and put on a good show but what more could he do faced with such overwhelming evidence?

Baxendale could feel that Egerton was now completely exposed with nowhere to go but she still had to choose her wording carefully to be sure of achieving the desired result.

"It is not a very laudable position for the Foreign Office to be in," she suggested.

"You are correct, but remember, it was advised to us by Mr Cassey; for whatever reason, I cannot understand why," replied Egerton in a blustering manner, trying desperately to divert some of the blame on to Customs.

"Success," she must have thought. A sense of satisfaction and elation seemed to spread over her. I admired her preparation and attention to detail – she knew her brief well and had prepared the questions very carefully. Baxendale had persuaded Egerton to concede that the Foreign Office were in the wrong but what choice was there, given Nixon's note?

Egerton was now looking distinctly uneasy while Baxendale leaned back, relaxing a little, ready to allow Scott the final moments of the drama to explore the question of Egerton's own complicity in the plot. Egerton was desperately hoping for some relief from this interminable suffering, Scott felt it was time for him to intervene to find out how much Egerton knew about the plan to interfere with the witnesses. The interrogation was still far from over.

"It was hoped to persuade the ambassador to decline to waive immunity so as to enable witnesses to appear whom the defence wanted to appear. It was suggested that Foreign Office officials approached the ambassadors to achieve this result. Up to what level would a suggestion of that sort go for approval?" asked Scott.

"This seemed to have gone to the head of department," replied Egerton, who was now perspiring profusely, the beads of sweat visible on his forehead.

And then Scott seized the moment to ask the ultimate question. Looking over his glasses towards Egerton and fixing him with a judicial stare, he gently probed: "Would it go to you?"

"I certainly have not seen this," responded Egerton firmly and resolutely.

But Scott was not prepared to be diverted so easily and persisted.

"Would you have expected it to have gone to you?"

"It would have been better if it had," said Egerton in an evasive and regretful manner.

Scott was now closing in, determined to get a direct answer to the important question of whether Egerton was knowingly involved in the plot.

"I think that probably means, yes, you would have expected it to have gone to you," insisted Scott.

I could see that Egerton seemed shaken and was clearly on the ropes this time. Attack would now be his best form of defence and, again, he seemed keen to put on a good show for his masters.

"Yes, because it was a bad case," he blustered. Egerton's tone was now becoming more robust. "I suppose the only slightly ameliorating factor is that we were looking forward to the prosecution of the English person involved, which is Major Dunk."

Scott and Baxendale were not best pleased by Egerton's response and the gloves were now off. Egerton's answer had offended all their beliefs in the rule of law and fair trial.

"It is not just Major Dunk; there were other defendants as well, and they wanted to rely on a defence that the Foreign Office and Customs and Excise were stopping them putting forward?" insisted Baxendale.

"Correct, yes," replied Egerton, sensing that perhaps he had overstepped the mark in his previous answer and was now worrying about the consequences and another Exocet attack from his interrogators.

"That is a matter for them, rather than for someone in the Foreign Office to decide on?" insisted Baxendale.

Scott was now keen to re-enter the fray and discover Egerton's role in the affair. So before Egerton could answer the last question, Scott dived in. "You have told me that this was not put before you for approval. Did you not know that this had happened until you saw these papers?"

"I am afraid not, no. I do not know how, but I did not. I must have been travelling or out of the country, or something like that," blustered Egerton.

Both interrogators could sense that their man was on the ropes once more, and this time there was no escape. The tension was rising to a climax and Baxendale jumped straight back in with another jab – invoking possibly one of the most important climaxes of the Scott Inquiry.

"Would you have expected it to come to you?" she pressed.

"Yes, I would have, actually," answered Egerton.

Scott had now heard quite enough and was keen to finish things his way. Looking directly at Egerton, he fixed him with a stern gaze.

"It seems to me, of course, looking at it as a lawyer, and not as a civil servant, as disgraceful. Do you find anything to object to in that adjective?"

Egerton sensed that the end was now in sight and he should tread carefully. But no matter how bad the misconduct, all his instincts told him to hold his nerve a little longer and not give way – his masters would not be pleased were he to accept such a damning indictment.

"I would say it was a bad show," muttered Egerton apologetically.

So there it was. The interrogation was now over: the officials had stopped the witnesses from appearing at trial and Nixon had admitted that the plan amounted "to connive at impeding the course of justice." One would have expected this plan to have come to

Egerton's notice but apparently he was unaware of it at the time. Egerton had congratulated Customs and dismissed the misconduct simply as "a bad show".

I had actually preferred Scott's more appropriate adjective, "disgraceful". The revelations that afternoon were staggering and what Scott had been able to unearth was unbelievable. And what would Reg Dunk make of all of this? Was this really the British justice that I had had drilled into me and had always respected throughout my life?

And so began the next stage of my twenty-five-year struggle for justice. I would certainly never forget 15 June 1993. It had been a seminal day. However, as events were to turn out, it would still take another fifteen years for justice finally to be done.

Chapter 20

Machinations

Dunk and I had spoken at length about the revelations spilling out of the Egerton inquisition and more importantly about what could be done now. Dunk was incandescent to hear what had actually happened and was now "out to get them bastards."

There was also public concern over the officials' behaviour. *The Times* had featured on 29 September 1993 a full letter written by Dunk headed, "Seeking redress in arms-for-Iraq case". In this, Dunk drew parallels between the Matrix Churchill and his own case. He had been a victim of what had appeared to him to be an attempt to pervert the course of justice.

> Whereas the Matrix Churchill affair is obviously of far greater national significance, the comments by Lord Justice Scott last June about my conviction should not be overlooked. The two are cast in the same mould.
>
> From the evidence given at the Scott Inquiry this year it seems that my company and I were the victims of what appears to have been an attempt to pervert the course of justice, involving Customs and Excise and the Foreign and Commonwealth Office, by way of bringing diplomatic pressure on some of our defence witnesses just days before the trial. I was advised at the very last minute by counsel that there was absolutely no option but to change our plea to guilty.
>
> Lord Justice Scott said in June that that collusion was "disgraceful". The FCO official, Sir Stephen Egerton, who was being interrogated about it and other matters, agreed it was

"a bad show". I, of course, had no knowledge that the witnesses had been interfered with until it was revealed in the Scott Inquiry (for which I am very grateful).

As a result, I have already taken the first steps to overturn the verdict and seek appropriate damages....

Armed with the transcript of the Scott Inquiry, Dunk's lawyers lost no time in marching off to the Appeal Court to put the record straight rather than waiting for the publication of the full Scott Report, which was not due to be published until 1996. At seventy-four, Dunk was not getting any younger and couldn't afford to hang on indefinitely. The compensation process could drag on for years.

As a result of the new evidence that had emerged from the Scott Inquiry, Dunk and Schlesinger were granted permission to appeal out of time against their conviction. Although they had pleaded guilty, it was clear that they had intended to contest the case and had offered their guilty plea only after the witnesses had failed to attend the trial and the indication that there would be no prison sentence.

The grounds of the appeal were that there had been an abuse of process arising from "two separate and serious improprieties of the prosecuting authorities".

Firstly, it was submitted that Customs "through the Foreign Office deliberately interfered with potential witnesses or manipulated affairs through the foreign embassies so as to prevent defence witnesses, who would otherwise have given evidence ... from being allowed to come to court at all. They thereby deliberately prevented the appellants from having a fair trial."

Secondly, it was submitted that had the trial judge been made aware of the contact with the embassies, he would have stayed the case as an abuse of process.

The hearing of the appeal was set down for 28 July 1994. The date of 15 June 1993 had already been heavily etched on my mind following the Egerton revelations, and 28 July 1994 was also to be a memorable date.

The outcome was obviously important for Dunk and Schlesinger.

But it was significant for me as well. If successful, it would show that I was also denied a fair trial.

The morning of the hearing was quite normal for me at chambers. I had become quite accustomed to absorbing the flak of panicking red-eyed barristers rushing off to courts everywhere, complaining about their bloody clerks never getting fees in on time, instructing solicitors who were incompetent and incapable of delivering papers promptly, and irate judges barking at them because they were unprepared – forgetting their own days at the Bar, of course.

So, on a sunny July morning, I sneaked out of the snake pit that was chambers to stroll along Middle Temple Lane towards the Strand for the hearing at the Royal Courts of Justice.

The RCJ is a large grey stone edifice in the late Victorian Gothic style, designed by George Edmund Street, a solicitor turned architect. As any user would tell you, only a lawyer could have designed such an impractical and inaccessible building.

Along the Strand, there was the usual procession of lawyers heading towards that great debating chamber. Silks (Queen's Counsel wearing silk robes) were being followed by their juniors and their long-suffering clerks trundling trolleys laden with bundles of documentary verbiage tied up in red tape. In their wake followed flustered solicitors and unwitting clients, unaware of the true cost of what often turned out to be fruitless ventures. The great myth in law is that there are winners and losers, whereas often there are no winners, except lawyers, to be sure.

Cautiously crossing the road, this time taking great care to avoid the traffic, there was the usual scene of protestors waving placards and the paparazzi, but not yet for me. I strode through the revolving doors and past the security checks to examine the daily cause lists.

This was a very embarrassing political case and the stakes could be high. Though acquitted, I was hoping that a successful appeal would amount to complete exoneration for me – if the goods were a gift to Jordan, there was no case. A successful appeal would also improve the prospects of financial redress.

I scanned the list hoping that the tribunal would be fair and not too prosecution-minded. So it was a relief to discover that Lord Chief Justice Taylor – Britain's top judge – would be presiding, with Mr Justice Ognall and Mr Justice Gage. The late Peter Taylor was known to be a fair man. An establishment judge with ambition may have viewed the officials' behaviour and the consequential embarrassment in an entirely different light.

The Lord Chief was a northerner who, after attending the Royal Grammar School in Newcastle, had read law at Cambridge. It was thought that perhaps his highest profile case was the prosecution in 1979 of the then Liberal Party Leader, Jeremy Thorpe, for conspiracy to murder.

Though all defendants were acquitted, Taylor won praise for his fair handling of the case. He also had prosecuted in the cases of Judith Ward and Stefan Kiszko, two of the most notorious miscarriage of justice cases of the twentieth century, which had led to the Police and Criminal Evidence Act 1984 (PACE) to improve the chances of fair trial.

Perhaps Lord Taylor's experience of such cases had convinced him that similar cases would come to light and of the importance of the prosecution giving full disclosure. Immediately upon his appointment in February 1992, he took the unprecedented step of calling a press conference saying he would like people to feel that British justice is the best in the world.

So after the collapse of the Matrix Churchill trial, there had been a great deal of concern among the judiciary about the case, especially the misuse of Public Interest Immunity (PII) certificates, known as 'gagging orders', and the resulting loss of faith in the courts. Thus he was an eminently suitable judge to rule. I hoped that he would take this opportunity to re-enforce the message about the importance of full disclosure and the right to fair trial in order to help restore confidence in the courts.

I slipped into Court Number 1 to listen in. My immediate reaction was to look towards the bench and at the three bewigged judges. There was the usual scene in the Lord Chief's Court as Crown Counsel was addressing the tribunal. Looking around the room were Dunk and Schlesinger, seated behind their legal teams and completely absorbed by the proceedings. Godfrey Carey QC had been instructed to represent them.

While taking a seat behind them, I caught sight of my original prosecuting counsel, Anthony Arlidge QC, now leading for the Crown in the appeal. Suddenly, visions of the original trial, with him having crudely waved a Sterling before the jury some nine years earlier, flooded back. Quite coincidentally after that trial, we had bumped into each other and had travelled together on the Birmingham train. We chatted continuously and I recall thinking what a decent chap he was. The Bar certainly does seem to attract those who are able to play many parts.

Arlidge now addressed the bench with a summary of the government's position. It was surprising that, notwithstanding Scott's findings and the incontrovertible misconduct of the officials, the government was still determined to contest the appeal at any cost.

The government's point was that the guilty pleas should not be set aside irrespective of the misconduct. Customs may have been prepared to take technical points but their counsel was less sanguine. Keen to disassociate himself from such a disgraceful position, Arlidge conceded defiantly: "M'Lud, it is not my role to defend the indefensible." This was a staggering admission by any stretch of the imagination from the government's mouthpiece.

Such a realistic concession was welcomed by the judges. They seemed to look at Arlidge rather more sympathetically than at his clients, in the knowledge that much as he would try to put on a brave face for his masters, it would be impossible to uphold such a conviction.

Given the officials' behaviour and the defendants' ignorance of it, the judges did not appear to be terribly attracted to, or much impressed by, Customs' submissions. In the end, the Lord Chief had little difficulty in granting the appeal. In doing so, a clear message was sent to express the court's displeasure about the officials' behaviour.

"In our judgment, the machinations in this case to prevent witnesses for the defence being available, coupled with the non-disclosure of what had been done, constituted such an interference with the justice process as to amount to an abuse of it," said Lord Taylor.

He then addressed the appellants somewhat apologetically: "Mr Dunk and Mr Schlesinger, I am now formally quashing your convictions, and the fines and legal costs of the trial and appeal will be repaid."

So there it was; the convictions had been quashed unanimously without any hesitation – eleven years after arrest and nine years after trial. It had not taken long for the Appeal Court to condemn the officials' behaviour as "machinations" and an interference with the course of justice, and to quash the convictions.

Justice had finally been done, thanks to Sir Richard Scott and Lord Taylor. Dunk and Schlesinger were obviously delighted; there was much to celebrate and a crowd of well-wishers gathered around them. But there was no time for me to join in as I had to rush back to chambers.

The atmosphere on the other side of the court seemed distinctly subdued as Arlidge tried his best to commiserate with Customs. No doubt there would be much reflection and concern about how this would be reported and the ensuing public vilification. Armies of civil servants would now be working through the night to brief ministers on the outcome, the line to take and how to minimize the embarrassment.

Perhaps the Iraqi and Jordanian Embassies would be none too pleased either about the outcome and publication of their role in the government plot. Clearly, Customs had dropped everyone in it, well and truly, again. There would be no promotions or knighthoods this time. In fact, given that Lord Taylor had referred the case to the CPS for investigation into the officials' behaviour, there must have been fear and panic amongst the officials concerned and all around Whitehall. And, of course, also, there must have been a great deal of concern about how much Lord Justice Scott would censure Whitehall in his report. In fact, given that Lord Taylor had referred the case to the CPS for investigation into the officials' behaviour, there must have been fear and panic amongst the officials concerned and all around Whitehall. And, of course, also, there must have been a great deal of concern about how much Lord Justice Scott would censure Whitehall in his report.

I was pleased that the outcome was positive for me, but the pleasure was all too short-lived. Still in a state of financial turmoil, living one day to the next, I wondered how I would survive and how I could continue to pay schools fees for my four children. As I left court and made my way through the gathered crowd, my mind drifted back over all the events of the past ten years and wondered when the nightmare would finally end.

My reverie abruptly ended with my return to chambers that afternoon. I was greeted by the usual barrage of messages and barristers' demands for still more work and collection of their fees. Out of the blue, I received a call from Dunk. "Is that young James?"

This was a most welcome call, and a relief from the madhouse of chambers that brought a smile to my face. Reg sounded elated. He was in very good form and always amused me with his particular brand of humour.

"Reg, it's you; how very good to hear you, now a 'free' man. Sorry that I had to rush back to chambers. I'd like to congratulate you on the appeal – you must be delighted after all you've been through. But what are you going to do now?"

"I don't know, but one thing is for sure, all those bastards are really going to pay for what they've done to me. Anyway, let's have a chat about this, son. I'd like to ask you to lunch next Wednesday at Simpson's, where we can get some proper English fayre; none of that foreign muck!"

Dunk's determination "to beat the bastards" did not surprise me, and I chuckled at his appreciation for all things English.

"And I'd like to introduce you to a new young fella who'll be workin' on my compensation."

"Really? Who's that? Which London firm is he at?" I enquired, assuming that Dunk had hired a top City lawyer.

"Nay, lad, not one of them lot. And he seems quite a bit smarter than the usual dozy flock up north. You'll like him. He's at a small

London firm representing the Matrix Churchill lot and he's a persistent little Mancunian shit."

"Oh no," I groaned, "not another bloody northerner with the usual music-hall lilt?"

"That's enough of your lip, son; he may even do you some good – you never know. But there again, I've had a number of bloody useless lawyers in my time so let's hope he's not one of them."

"Yeah, I should know about useless lawyers," I echoed with some feeling.

"Well, son, it just doesn't seem right to me that I get compensation but you get nowt when you've lost far more than me, haven't ya?" mused Dunk.

"Thanks, Reg. I accept lunch with alacrity, and am looking forward to seeing you on Wednesday and to meeting your 'hot-shot lawyer'. It would be terrific if he could help me in any way – it's so kind of you to think of me. You know, Reg, you're right – I've lost a lot, including the sale of Sterling. And, I often feel even sadder about my 150 loyal employees who all lost their jobs needlessly when Sterling was shut down," I said with regret.

That evening, on my way home along the Strand, I picked up a copy of the *Evening Standard* as I dived into Temple tube station. As I flicked through it I noticed a headline: "FO 'abused the law' in Arms-for-Iraq trial". So the appeal had indeed made the news and the headline said it all.

I glanced over the opening paragraph:

GOVERNMENT interference with defence witnesses and a subsequent cover-up in an "Arms-for-Iraq" trial were branded an unlawful abuse of the justice system by Britain's top judge today. The Lord Chief Justice, Lord Taylor, said Foreign Office intervention that prevented key witnesses from giving evidence was "disgraceful".

A feeling of satisfaction came over me. At least the officials' behaviour had now been exposed publicly and this was some vindication at last. But the satisfaction was short-lived in the absence of any public apology or even any sign of regret, and some compensation, of course.

The Daily Telegraph and *The Independent* also reported the Appeal Court decision the following day, 29 July 1996. *The Telegraph* reported that:

> Lord Taylor's censure of the government was unprecedented and the judgment astonished MPs on both sides of the Commons and led to calls for an inquiry. Dr John Cunningham, Shadow Foreign Secretary, said, "If any ordinary member of the public interfered with witnesses in a trial, they would find themselves accused of trying to pervert the course of justice. It is a scandal and the taxpayer is left once again footing the bill for this abuse of power." Sir Nicholas Bonsor, Conservative MP for Upminster and Chairman of the Commons Select Committee, said any interference by a government department in the judicial process was "unacceptable".

The Independent banner headline concluded that:

> Arab embassies were persuaded to silence defence witnesses, Court of Appeal told.

The *Daily Mail* headline put it plainly:

> An abuse of justice
> Judge condemns civil servants who silenced arms witnesses

That said it all.

The days passed by slowly at chambers as I looked forward to the celebratory lunch with Dunk. The duly appointed day arrived. I appeared at Simpson's early. I liked the place enormously, as my father used to take me there as a boy and it had not changed at all. The menu still sported the H.M. Bateman cartoon of the reaction of horror by the staff when a diner enquired as to whether the meat was English or foreign.

I was ushered to the table that Reg had booked and sat down to take in fully the surrounding scene and the memories of it. What would my staid and respectable father have thought of my roller-coaster life? There exuded a truly warm atmosphere. Then Reg appeared with a much younger man following in his trail.

"Hello, son. Glad you could make it. Are those legal bastards treating you well?" Before I could pass comment on my stable of barristers, Dunk blustered on. "This here is young Lawrence, Lawrence Kormornick, who's now my lawyer."

I shook hands with Kormornick, smiled and nodded in the traditional fashion. He did likewise. Dunk always brought a hint of amusement and bonhomie to anything in which he participated, including arms dealing. That's why the Arabs liked him. Ironically, here he was now with a Jew.

I have a propensity to try and associate the appearance of a stranger with someone in the public eye so that it is easy to describe him to others. I immediately thought that the youthful-looking Kormornick, with his sparkling green eyes, resembled a cross between Daniel Craig – later to become James Bond – and Vladimir Putin. When I mentioned the likeness, it caused Kormornick to grin, especially as he claimed to be of Russian descent.

After the niceties and during the excellent lunch, which would have wreaked havoc with the cholesterol count of any normal human being, Reg suggested that Kormornick might be able to do me some good.

Kormornick explained that he was hoping to recover some compensation for Dunk under a government statutory scheme for wrongful conviction.

"But you were acquitted, so that scheme wouldn't apply to you," he told me, sympathetically.

"Unfortunately, as it has turned out, I was acquitted, so I'm not quite sure where that leaves me. I've also been thinking about having a go at Customs and the Foreign Office, but that's not cheap, especially without legal aid," I sighed.

"Frankly, I don't fancy your chances of that very much. You see, the law in this area is quite tricky and very expensive – and the government has much deeper pockets than you. Perhaps it's best to wait for the Scott Report first to see if that helps. However, there is a government ex-gratia scheme for wrongful charge that you could try, which is a much cheaper option. Given the Appeal Court Ruling you should satisfy the serious default requirement. But the custody criterion is the real challenge because you were on unconditional bail and were never remanded in custody. It's a bit of a long shot but it's worth a try, so don't give up hope just yet," explained Kormornick.

I listened carefully as he outlined what he could do for me.

"I don't hold out any promises, but I'd like to investigate the possibilities of getting some compensation for you. It's very remote, and I may end up doing lots of work for nothing, but I have some ideas. I'm already working on a similar case, and we can run yours on a flexible basis, if you like."

"What do you mean?" I queried suspiciously, as my vast experience with the legal fraternity knew bitterly that somewhere along the line, the lay client is always milked like a cow. "Are you sure? And could you also have a chat with my lawyers about Customs and the Foreign Office?" I queried, not believing that I would not be charmingly relieved of some sizeable retainer.

Thus was born an interesting association.

There was to be more embarrassment for the government in November 1995, when Lord Taylor also quashed the convictions in the Ordtec case.

Paul Grecian and others (known as the 'Ordtec 4') had been convicted of being involved in supplying arms to Iraq and received suspended sentences. They had been advised to plead guilty bereft of vital documents showing government knowledge after Judge Spence upheld the government's PII certificates and ruled that those documents were irrelevant to the case. The charges against John Grecian (Paul Grecian's father) were dropped. However, after the spectacular collapse of the Matrix Churchill case in November 1992, and the revelations about government knowledge of trade with Iraq, the Ordtec 4 filed an appeal.

Geoffrey Robertson QC, who had pulled off a famous victory in Matrix Churchill three years earlier, was the obvious choice to lead for the appellants. To the rescue came Lord Taylor, who once again was not greatly impressed by the behavior of the government or their appeal submissions. He held that they had been denied a fair trial because the government had withheld vital documents about government knowledge of exports to Iraq. There was some concern about the misuse of PII certificates and this would be a recurrent theme in the Scott Report.

It was revealed at the appeal that Grecian had also been working as a Special Branch informer and was the first person to inform Whitehall that Iraq was building a "supergun" with the help of British companies. Despite that, he was investigated and prosecuted by HM Customs and Excise.

So it turned out that the government decided to abandon Grecian just as they had with Paul Henderson, the MD of Matrix Churchill, although both were brave men who had risked their lives to serve their country. There was great concern in government that Grecian could run a defence at trial that they knew about the exports from his intelligence reports, and that this was to be avoided if at all possible. In August 1990, a Foreign Office official apparently compiled a briefing note for the security services that said:

> If Ordtec ends up in court [Mr Grecian] may be persuaded to keep quiet about his connections with [Special Branch] and yourselves but there is an obvious risk he will try the "working for British intelligence" ploy.

The official added:

> His personal future might be in some doubt if he was ever publicly identified as the man who blew the [whistle] on the Iraqi Babylon project. If we were not too squeamish, we might use this point to ensure silence.

During the appeal, it emerged that the prosecution had told Grecian at his trial they could not protect him from possible recriminations from the IRA, on whom he had also informed, or from the Iraqis, if he refused to plead guilty.

Henderson and Grecian were no doubt aware of the serious risks they were taking in revealing their intelligence roles and the great danger to them and their families. They must have been sick with worry. What must they have said to their loved ones? It reminded me of just how worried I was about reprisals after the *Daily Express* article. It seemed to me to be inexplicable and inexcusable that they should have been put at risk, especially given what they had done for their country.

Of particular relevance to my case, the Appeal Court also ruled that the government had turned "a blind eye" towards the export of arms to Iraq via Jordan. A telegram from the British Embassy in Amman to the Foreign Office, on 28 May 1990, had said:

> Are we trying to ensure that the problem does not arise again by putting a stop to further Jordanian involvement in Iraqi procurement? Have we not turned a blind eye to Jordanian involvement in the past? (The Ambassador thinks that this has been the case.)

In 1996, the Home Secretary agreed to pay compensation to the Ordtec 4 under the wrongful conviction scheme, but there was still no chance for John Grecian and me under the wrongful charge scheme.

Chapter 21

Scott Reports

After Egerton appeared at the Scott Inquiry and the Appeal Court had finally put things right, I patiently awaited publication of the Scott Report, hoping that the findings could help me obtain a remedy in some way.

After some two years, the report was finally published in February 1996.

Scott and his team had been presented with a formidable task to obtain evidence, to conduct interviews, and then to write a report running into several volumes. More than 200 witnesses had submitted written evidence and over sixty were interviewed in more than eighty days of public hearings. A further fifteen witnesses gave evidence in secret sessions (mainly members of the security and intelligence agencies).

Scott commented on the difficulty of extracting from government departments the required documents (some 200,000 in all) and noted how Customs & Excise could not find out what Ministry of Defence policy was and how intelligence reports were not passed on to those who needed to know.

It was obvious that the cost of such an inquiry would not be inexpensive. According to a parliamentary response to a written question, a Mr Freeman confirmed in July 1996 that the total cost to public funds of the inquiry was £6,945,000.

The Report was published with two CD-ROM discs. This was the first time that CD-ROMs had been issued for an official inquiry. Unfortunately, however, the CD-ROMs did not include correspondence between Lord Justice Scott and current and former ministers and most of the evidence from the security services. Though the ministerial documents barred from inspection for thirty years at the Public Records Office in Kew eventually may be released, the secret services files will remain forever blocked.

Though most interest had focused on the Matrix Churchill case, obviously I was more interested in my own.

According to Richard Norton-Taylor, the author of *Truth is a Difficult Concept: Inside the Scott Inquiry* (1995):

> The government picked Lord Justice Scott for the job to avoid charges that it had chosen a compliant judge. It hoped, nevertheless, he would conduct a narrow inquiry, that he would give the government the benefit of the doubt. The government's gamble did not pay off.... The inquiry slowly undressed Whitehall, exposing incompetence, dissembling, dishonesty, a patronizing approach to Parliament and – perhaps worst of all – unacceptable interference in a criminal prosecution.... Whitehall will do its utmost to ensure that never again will a judge be given such freedom to conduct a public inquiry into the activities of government.

Lord Justice Scott lambasted Customs in the Matrix Churchill case over late disclosure of government documents showing that it knew about and had encouraged the exports and the misuse of Public Interest Immunity Certificates. But arguably his worst censure of the whole report was reserved for Customs and the Foreign Office in the Dunk case.

There was written evidence to the inquiry from the authors of some of the Foreign Office minutes concerning Customs' request to approach the embassies not to waive diplomatic immunity. Subpoenas requiring the attendance of witnesses could not, of course, have been used for the embassy witnesses because of diplomatic immunity. In answer to the question from the inquiry, "Do you accept that, in so doing, you are conniving at impeding the course of justice?" Mr Pigott replied:

I accept that this would be a reasonable construction to place on my action, if, by so doing, I would be frustrating the intention of the prosecution authority to bring a prosecution or secure a conviction. That, however, was not my intention. I repeat that, in passing on that message at the time, I was acting in good faith.

But Lord Justice Scott was not too impressed with this explanation and concluded that:

The intended effect of the overtures to the embassies was to deprive the defendants of the ability to call the embassy staff witnesses. It is, obviously, as much an impeding of the course of justice to frustrate defendants by interfering with defence witnesses as it is to frustrate the prosecution by interfering with prosecution witnesses. I do not believe that either Mr Nixon or Mr Pigott could have supposed otherwise. Indeed, the manuscript note from Mr Nixon to Mr Pigott refers to his "reluctance to connive at impeding the course of justice."

There was also written evidence submitted to the Inquiry from Mr Knox, a Customs Investigation Officer. Lord Justice Scott asked him why he considered it to be part of his function, as a Customs Investigation Officer, "to deter ambassadors from giving evidence as defence witnesses." In his written response to the Inquiry, Mr Knox said:

It was not at all clear at that stage how any evidence from the embassies would finally turn out and whether it would support either defence of prosecution contentions. We had not been able to question the embassy staff closely ... about their involvement or evident inconsistencies with a view either to seeking witness statements or establishing any complicity in the offences under investigation. At that time we did not believe that the embassies would be able to offer any tangible evidence to support the unlikely version of events suggested by some of the diplomatic staff....

I was convinced that some way should be explored to bring to the attention of the ambassadors the inconsistencies in the stories put forward and, by so doing, to open up a way for them and their staff to provide supporting evidence or to offer some other explanation. We could have pressed this directly with the embassies, but given the sensitive diplomatic factors, thought it better to involve the FCO....

I was therefore suggesting to the FCO the prudence of bringing the contradictory evidence to the attention of the ambassadors to discourage the embassy staff from putting forward inaccurate and unsubstantiated information ... which could eventually prove embarrassing to the ambassadors themselves and the governments of Iraq and Jordan. I do accept that this action could have deterred individuals from eventually putting forward false testimony.

Neither was Lord Justice Scott much persuaded by this explanation and concluded that:

The story that had emerged from the embassy staff may well have seemed an "unlikely version of events" that was "inaccurate and unsubstantiated" and contained "inconsistencies". But it was a matter for the jury to decide at the trial. It was not for Mr Knox, nor for any FCO officials, to seek to dissuade the embassy staff from giving the evidence. In his written statement, Mr Knox "rejected most strongly the suggestion that [he] was in any way attempting to impede the course of justice." But how else can his suggestion to Mr Wogan that the ambassadors should be "confronted with the contradictory evidence in our possession ... in the hope that this will deter them from taking a potentially embarrassing course of action" be interpreted? The terms of the letter, coupled with Mr Knox's explanation in his written statement, suggest that Mr Knox's objective was to bring about a situation in which evidence of an intended 'gift' of the 200 sub-machine guns to Jordan could not be given by embassy personnel because their respective ambassadors would not permit it.

Mr Knox in written comments to the Inquiry put forward another explanation for the terms of his letter to the FCO seeking assistance. The investigation was still in its early stages. The account given by the Iraqi Ambassador was inconsistent with other evidence that Customs had obtained.

> In any similar case where diplomatic immunity was not involved, we would have pursued our investigations with the authors of the gift story to test the evidence and to establish the facts: either that the gift story was true and corroborative evidence could be adduced, or that it was false and consideration had to be given to joining them in a conspiracy with Dunk....
>
> It was incumbent on us to consider how to pursue the matter by testing the Ambassador's oral statement....
>
> At the risk of belabouring the point, the only action being contemplated was to let the ambassadors see the evidence in our possession "in the hope" that they, of their own volition – not through any coercion or pressure – would drop any ideas they might have had about giving what we believed to be false evidence.

The thrust of this explanation was that Customs ID wanted to investigate the evidence to be given by the embassies and was hoping to discourage the giving of perjured evidence. Lord Justice Scott acknowledged that Mr Knox's explanation may be the correct one and that his letter of 25 February 1983 may have been "ineptly worded". But if the intention was to deter the embassies from giving evidence it was in the opinion of Lord Justice Scott, "totally unacceptable".

The report reinforced the fact that Lord Justice Scott was not greatly impressed by the officials' behaviour in the Dunk case.

Egerton's description that it was "a bad show" was an understatement. Customs' own barrister, Anthony Arlidge QC, had described their behaviour as "indefensible". In Lord Justice Scott's opinion, the behaviour of the Foreign Office officials was "disgraceful" and "reprehensible". However, Scott regarded the conduct of Customs as deserving of greater censure than that of the Foreign Office officials, stating:

> As the prosecutor in the case, it was Customs' duty to play its part in ensuring, or trying to ensure, that the defendants had a fair trial…. The failure to inform the defendants (or the court) of what had happened meant that neither the defendants nor the court were aware that a fair trial had been impeded…. If Customs ID had had worries about the nature of implications of the defence proposed to be run by the defendants, they should have shared them with the Customs solicitors…. An important question is why Customs ID did not do so….

Some may say that Customs ID was on the receiving end of what was arguably the most serious censure of the whole Scott Report. Others may say that they were indeed fortunate to have escaped an inquiry into the failure to 'inform the defendants (or the court) of what had happened….'

The significance of this was not lost on Lord Justice Taylor, who had slated Customs in Dunk's appeal for the failure to disclose to us what had happened.

Lord Justice Scott flagged up an important question as to why Customs had kept its solicitors, us and the court in the dark but so far there has never been an explanation. However, he accepted that there was no evidence before the Inquiry suggesting that the impropriety of Customs ID was known to anyone in its Solicitor's Office.

He was surprised that Customs ID was reluctant to share its concerns about the gift defence with its own solicitors and did not seek legal advice as to what lawful steps, if any, might be taken to deal with it. If Customs ID thought that it had behaved lawfully regarding the witnesses, then it had nothing at all to fear from informing its solicitors, the defendants, and the trial judge. One also wonders whether the Foreign Office officials had bothered to consult their own lawyers about Customs' request to have "friendly words" with the embassies.

It seems that during the Scott Inquiry, Customs was spared the additional embarrassment of questions about this non-disclosure to its solicitors, the defendants and the trial judge. The fact is that Customs was under a strict duty to disclose to us and the court, the communications passing between it and the Foreign Office about the plan to block witnesses and action taken. Had it done so, the likelihood is that this prejudice preventing a fair trial would have been fatal to any prosecution.

In the end, it is hard to believe that there can be a credible answer to the important question of why Customs ID did keep everyone in the dark.

I also wondered why there was no mention in Chapter 5 of the Scott Report dealing with the Dunk case, of any written statement from the FCO official, Patrick Nixon, or to any oral evidence that he and/or any other officials may have given to the Inquiry. Perhaps in view of matters arising from the Court of Appeal ruling in the Dunk case, it was not considered appropriate to do so. Accordingly, it fell to Stephen Egerton at the Inquiry hearing to account for the officials' behaviour.

In relation to the use of Jordan as a conduit for Iraq, Scott concluded that:

> Government knowledge that Jordan was being used as a diversionary destination goes back at least to 1983…. In a Note dated 26 May 1983 on Security Service files, the comment was made that "In view of the restrictions imposed on the sale of war material to Iraq and Iran, Iraq has been using Jordan as an intermediary." The Note related to a contract for the supply of arms to Iraq. The contract was to be signed by the Jordanian Military Attaché in London [Scott Report E2.4 and E.25].

I wondered why the government prosecuted us if they knew in 1983, and probably much earlier, that Jordan was being used as a diversionary destination. Jordan may have been a good friend of Iraq, but was also a good friend of Britain. Why had officials blocked the witnesses to impede the gift defence if they thought they had such a good case against us? Perhaps the government was concerned that the embassy witnesses could blow the gaffe on arms to Iraq? If so, had the witnesses not been blocked, it may have been necessary to abandon the prosecution in order to avoid the truth coming out.

John Major commented on the Scott Report on 16 February 1996:

> I think Sir Richard has done a very thorough, very competent job and I am very grateful to him…. The report was about whether innocent men were going to be sent to jail by conspiracy and whether Saddam Hussein was being armed by the British Government. Those were the charges. They are comprehensively dismissed and I don't think you can overlook the fact that that was what the report was about. They have gone. There is no doubt that didn't happen. I am delighted at the outcome…. I think there are lessons to learn from Sir Richard's report. It is very comprehensive. It has shown up some shortcomings and mistakes and I shall take these very seriously.

The nation was shocked with this analysis, which was met with a fierce rebuttal by *The Independent* on 19 February 1996:

> The very nature of the government's response may prove more damaging and incriminating for John Major and his colleagues than the Scott Report itself. Friday morning's newspapers suggested that the government might have got off "Scot-free…." By reacting dismissively and arrogantly to the Scott Report, Mr Major and his ministers have dug the government a deeper hole than might otherwise have been the case. Public opinion is too astute to be bamboozled by such blatant avoidance of the issues.

In the House of Commons, the Scott Report was debated. The late Robin Cook MP (who was later to become Foreign Secretary) laid into the Conservatives on behalf of the opposition, having been given only three hours to read the report. Ian Lang, President of the Board of Trade, made a pitiful attempt to defend the Conservatives against the weight of all the findings.

At 10.45 pm on 26 February 1996, MPs went through the lobbies on the censure motion over the Scott Report. The government's winning margin was by one single vote. Notwithstanding Scott's criticism of various government officials, there would be no resignations and no prosecutions.

But the electorate would have their opportunity to show their displeasure, and did so in 1997, when New Labour swept into office. I did take some satisfaction in seeing MPs such as William Waldegrave, Malcolm Rifkind and Ian Lang lose their seats. Perhaps future historians would attribute the Conservatives' defeat partly to the impact of the Scott Report, their response to it and how Parliament had been misled over exports to Iraq.

The Economist commented that:

Sir Richard exposed an excessively secretive government machine riddled with incompetence, slippery with the truth and willing to mislead Parliament.

Richard Norton-Taylor was more direct:

The Arms-to-Iraq affair was one of the most seedy, dishonest, buck-passing episodes in the history of modern British government. Had the Matrix Churchill trial not collapsed, and documents ministers wanted to suppress not been disclosed, three men could have been jailed in a miscarriage of justice in which ministers and civil servants would have connived.

The Sun also captured the mood of the nation very well in its own inimitable take:

Politicians are just slippery, power-hungry opportunists who will use any legitimate device to save their necks.

Chapter 22

The Yellow Brick Road

Lawrence Kormornick had advised me over the difficulties of taking on Customs but at the same time had also described the Home Office Scheme as a "long shot". So, with the benefit of the Scott Report, it still seemed worth having a go at Customs if someone was prepared to take the case on.

"Mary Poppins", one of the barristers in my stable was thus described. The fragrant Miss Sarah Davies specialized in family law, except for the odd appearance in the criminal courts, most notable of which was the defence in a prosecution under the Dangerous Dogs Act. She had felt compelled to take the case only because it was being heard at, of all places, the Barking Magistrates' Court.

Sarah's husband, Martin Edwards, was a planning solicitor with Titmuss Sainer & Webb (later "& Dechert", and later still, the appellation of the whole was shortened to merely "Dechert"). My mother played bridge regularly with a Miss Sainer, who had told her that her late brother was the firm's founder and the private solicitor of the well-known tycoon, Sir Charles Clore.

I had been invited to dinner with Sarah Davies and Martin Edwards immediately after the quashing of the Dunk conviction, and naturally the case became the topic of conversation. Martin was absolutely insistent on taking me into the firm in Serjeants' Inn, because they were familiar with Customs & Excise. He felt strongly that his wife's clerk had been hard done by.

"Come on round and I'll introduce you to Gavin McFarlane and Malachi Cornwell-Kelly [who were ex-Customs lawyers]. Since they are specialists in Customs & Excise work, they might relish a bit of the gamekeeper turned poacher."

An appointment was arranged to meet with Gavin McFarlane, a personable, healthy-looking man with a tanned face like a walnut. He was actually a barrister in full-time employment with the company. He thought that the wrongful charge scheme was hopeless and that, "no lawyer in his right mind would be prepared to take it on." I explained my position and hastened to add the rider, "but I am chronically short of funds."

"Never mind, we'll keep costs to a minimum, but we'll certainly get you something. By the way, who are the people that you've come across in Customs?" enquired McFarlane.

I reeled off the names of all the investigators, all of whom McFarlane knew. "Oh yes, I nearly forgot; we went to see Mr Silverstone to try to stop all this."

"Silverstone? Never heard of him."

And so began an action against Customs & Excise and the Foreign Office for personal loss, business loss and all the court costs. The case was based on the officials' misbehaviour in stopping the defence witnesses from coming to court – in legal terms described as "conspiracy and misfeasance in public office". The claim was based on the incontrovertible findings of the Appeal and the Scott Inquiry – evidence enough to prove the case, one would have thought. After all, it's not often that four senior judges condemn the government.

I was naturally keen to find out the government's response and to get on with the case. However, as the wheels of justice grind forever slowly, I would have to wait some months.

The months passed by and eventually I received a telephone call from McFarlane.

"Hello, James, I've got some news for you."

"Hi, Gavin; it's good to hear from you at last. Is the news good? Are they going to do the decent thing?" I enquired.

"Umm, not exactly," McFarlane hesitated.

"Meaning?"

"Well, it's not going to be as straightforward as we first imagined. They're denying responsibility for everything, sorry. You'd better come in and see me for a chat."

"What! No responsibility at all? Disgraceful!"

"Ok, but I'll send you a copy of the defence. I'm not sure you're going to like it much and you'd better read it for yourself before we meet," insisted McFarlane.

I came off the telephone completely bemused, unable to understand how the government could possibly deny all responsibility given what the judges had said.

The following day, a manila envelope landed in chambers marked, "James Edmiston Esq – strictly private and confidential, addressee only".

I opened the envelope quickly as I was keen to read the defence. Most of it was in the usual obscure legalese that had kept the profession in business for centuries. It confirmed my belief that legal documents are verbose because lawyers charge by the word. But as I attempted to navigate through this veritable labyrinth of words, my attention was drawn to a particularly odd turn of phrase that claimed the officials "have absolute immunity from suit on the ground of public policy." Surely this was not some sort of attempt by the government to avoid its responsibility, I thought? I was right out of my depth. I'd have to ask McFarlane to "translate".

En route to McFarlane, I managed to dodge my barristers like some Harry Potter character flying through the Temple to Serjeants' Inn. At reception, I was greeted by a particularly attractive and friendly young lady who attended on me while I waited for McFarlane to appear. Surveying the lavish reception area that befitted their obviously "high net worth" clients, this appeared to me to be quite a different world from the sobriety of chambers.

As I was taking in the sumptuous surroundings, McFarlane suddenly appeared, assistant in tow, to greet me and usher me into one of the nearby conference rooms. It had never ceased to amaze me how lawyers tended to move in clusters at great expense to the soon-to-be impecunious client. After the initial traditional pleasantries, McFarlane got straight to the matter in question.

"James, I'm afraid it's not looking too good for you now. Sorry."

"For heaven's sake, what are you talking about? You originally said I had a strong case based on the Appeal Court and the Scott Inquiry. So what's suddenly changed?"

"Yes, well, the government has not been slow to latch on to a loophole from the recent Silcott case. Basically, they're claiming immunity from prosecution," sighed McFarlane.

"Sorry, I'm being a little slow, but what does that mean?"

"Yes, it's all a bit odd really. After Winston Silcott was cleared of the murder of PC Blakelock, he tried to claim compensation. Customs say that acting in the course of an investigation, it's public policy that they have no legal responsibility," McFarlane explained.

"You're joking; no responsibility? Are you saying that Customs can get away with misconduct during an investigation? That can't be right – can't we challenge this?" I insisted.

"Yes, but there are no guarantees, of course, and this could be a rather long and drawn-out affair and terribly expensive and uncertain – not easy taking on the establishment on technical legal points that could swing either way, you know."

I felt deflated. Once again, my hopes had hit the floor. So the government was saying that I could not sue the officials for "disgraceful" and "reprehensible" actions because they had immunity. The use of public policy against me to give the officials immunity just did not appear right to me. Why should someone who had suffered a gross injustice at the hands of senior public officials be left without any remedy? It added insult to injury. But what really irked me was the total absence of any sense of responsibility and the lack of any remorse.

That night I reflected carefully on my predicament. Clearly, the legal point was very technical and the civil court could take a very different view from the criminal court. It could even end up in the House of Lords. But I wanted none of that, of course. I was in no financial position to mount legal opposition against two government departments that could string out litigation to drown even the most affluent of opponents.

I also recalled the habitual ritual dances with the bursars of the various educational establishments attended by my four children at the beginning of each term so that they might be allowed back in. Their future education was already hanging by a thread. So the decision was beyond doubt; I simply couldn't afford to pursue the case any further, and so ended yet another false dawn.

The only consolation was that *The Guardian* followed the story closely, through Richard Norton-Taylor, and felt that its readers would be interested in the case. The edition on Saturday, 12 October 1996 carried the banner headline: "Iraq affair officials immune", and below that, "Alleged victims cannot sue civil servants for 'disgraceful' actions".

The Guardian piece was very supportive and reminded its readers of the findings of the Scott Inquiry and the Appeal Court. The piece also mentioned that Sir David Gilmore, Permanent Secretary at the Foreign Office, had subsequently reminded all staff of "the need unfailingly to observe the law of the land."

The article concluded by reporting that the Crown Prosecution Service had asked Scotland Yard to investigate the activities of Mr Pigott and Mr Nixon. There followed a protracted investigation.

We had been awaiting news of the investigation and Dunk had said this to a journalist:

> I am very encouraged to learn about the CPS report. This is the first piece of positive news that I have heard ... I thought the whole thing would just be dead and buried. My company and I were the victims of what appears to pervert [sic] the course of justice.... It is only when one gets into a situation like that one realizes just how ruthless and cynical the people at the top can be.

But on Christmas Eve 1996, the Crown Prosecution Service announced that they would not be prosecuted – clearly a good day to bury bad news when the mind of the populace focused on Christmas.

The Director of the Crown Prosecution Service, the late Dame Barbara Mills, had decided that no one criticized in the Scott Report would be prosecuted. Such conduct is apparently not unlawful, providing, of course, that those involved are senior government officials. To make matters worse, apparently some of the officials in my case had even gained promotion.

The *Daily Mail* had been covering the story closely and published an article about the CPS decision not to prosecute any of the officials under the title, "Officials in the clear over Iraq arms scandal":

Opposition spokesmen turned on the government yesterday after it was revealed that no criminal charges would be brought against officials accused in the "Arms-to-Iraq" affair.

The Crown Prosecution Service ruled that that an investigation into claims that Customs and Excise officers and Foreign Office staff conspired to prevent a fair trial of company directors accused of illegal exports had not produced sufficient evidence.

This was despite forthright criticism from Sir Richard Scott over the so-called Dunk affair....

Labour Foreign affairs spokesman Robin Cook said: "If anybody should have been in the dock, it should have been the government.... Many officials knew only too well what was going on and appear to have been willing to cover it up."

The Liberal Democrats' defence and foreign affairs spokesman Menzies Campbell said: "It is no wonder the public regards politicians and the political system with such distaste when no one is willing to take either political or legal blame for the supply of arms to Iraq. This shameful episode and Scott's damaging criticism will be an enduring monument to eighteen years of Tory government."

That was probably how many were feeling about double standards and the officials being let off the hook.

It was at about this time that the payment or late payment of clerks' fees became a real problem. There were some issues about the level of fees recovered on assessment by me. So much so that on advice from the head of chambers, resort was taken to the chambers' solicitors to pursue the two worst malefactors.

The solicitor for the Institute of Barristers' Clerks was utterly successful in collecting my outstanding fees from other delinquent barristers, but he would not touch the cases already set in motion by the chambers' solicitors. Eventually, I was dumped by them as my credit ran out, and was left all alone to fight the professionals at their own game as a litigant in person.

Here I was, working flat-out in chambers during the day, and then having to prepare bundles for my own court hearings. It was really hard going, extremely stressful and only partially successful. The fees were almost insignificant compared with the costs, but I had made commitments to pay both school fees and a mortgage.

I finally left chambers to fight this case full-time. The last commitment of school fees had been paid, but the Inland Revenue was now chasing me, although they were most understanding about my predicament. I failed to be awarded costs, and was made liable for the astronomic costs of the litigation in the attempt to gain my just deserts.

This was a difficult period for me. But at least weekends were spent happily at Kiddington, the beautiful Oxfordshire estate where I rented a cottage from my good friend, Maurice Robson. I was surviving, but only just.

Chapter 23

Muck and Brass

By 1999, I was still in debt, my income was dwindling and I had no prospects of gainful employment. With no apparent chance of redress, the future looked rather bleak.

With the Customs case now abandoned, all my hopes were now riding on Dunk's Home Office case and any help from Kormornick. The Home Secretary, Michael Howard QC, had allowed Dunk into the wrongful conviction scheme in 1996 and for three years, Kormornick and Dunk had been totally immersed in preparing his compensation case.

The scheme allowed for written submissions only, with no oral hearing. There was no room for any error and the papers had to be in perfect order. Facts had to be supported by a mass of evidence and a voluminous expert accounting report (as I was later to discover myself). The only "appeal" was a challenge by way of judicial review, which would be difficult, if not impossible, and, of course, the legal costs would not be inconsiderable.

Not only had he endured a great deal of pain and suffering, Dunk had lost a successful business. Now approaching eighty, time was quickly running out for him. His health and that of his wife had deteriorated enormously as a direct result of the worry and stress in the years from 1983.

But by June 1999, the waiting would finally be over. After fighting for sixteen years, Dunk was finally awarded record compensation of more than £2 million. The award was made by the Home Secretary, Jack Straw, on the advice of the Independent Assessor, Sir David Calcutt QC, now deceased.

The media had picked up on the size of the award. This was substantially more than other victims' awards. This caused uproar amongst those who had been imprisoned for years, because Dunk had never been in prison. It was splashed all over the papers and the Internet, to the embarrassment of the authorities.

The award gave hope to others like me who had suffered a gross miscarriage of justice. Dunk always believed, "If you can stick it out and you have a good case, you will win through. You may not come out of it unscathed, but it may be worth it, just to know you have beaten the bastards."

But it wasn't all plain sailing for Dunk either. Though the Home Office had compensated him personally, they were not prepared to compensate the company for its losses. Never being one to back down, the company then challenged the refusal by way of judicial review but was unsuccessful – the court ruled that the compensation scheme only applied to individuals. The wider significance of this landmark ruling was that companies that suffer financial loss because they are victims of miscarriage of justice cannot be awarded compensation from the government.

The Times was also interested in the story and published another letter from Dunk in March 1997 entitled, "Human cost of 'Arms-to-Iraq' affair":

> In July 1994, I and my company, Atlantic Commercial UK Ltd, won our appeal against our convictions in 1985 for alleged illegal export of arms to Iraq, because of information dredged up from FCO files by Sir Richard Scott when preparing his report into the Matrix-Churchill affair....
>
> The results of the conviction, apart from fines, costs and confiscation, were the virtual ruin of my company and the enforced dismissal of its staff. It ruined my life, a penalty far in excess of that intended, I am sure, by the court in 1985.
>
> Whereas the Home Office have agreed to compensate me for my personal loss ... they maintain it does not provide for compensation for miscarriages of justice against "companies".

The only redress is to sue the original prosecuting authority, HM Customs, but since I am seventy-seven and my company has been ruined, how can it afford to?... Is this the British justice we were all taught to regard so highly?

Dunk and I enjoyed a celebratory meal at Simpson's (of course). He talked with great excitement about all his plans to cruise the Western Isles in his new boat. It had always been a great source of regret that his previous much-loved motor yacht had been sold to fund his defence costs. But that was all behind him and the future was now looking rosy, or so he thought.

Though there was little cheer for me, I tried to put on a brave face having always received much support and encouragement from Dunk, who sympathized with my predicament. Perhaps he may have been slightly embarrassed that the Jordan order had got me into all this mess and that I was uncompensated.

Dunk was very keen to find out how I was getting on with my own efforts to secure some compensation and was sorry to hear that I was not having much success. It seemed so unfair that he should qualify under the wrongful conviction scheme yet I was ineligible under the wrongful charge scheme, given that both cases were so similar. But Dunk was optimistic and had a great deal of faith in Kormornick. His advice was that if I could stick it out, I would eventually "beat the bastards."

It was a also a great source of regret to Dunk and me that, apart from the Home Office award, neither Customs nor the Foreign Office, or any of the officials, had been held to account, and that neither of us had received an apology. But now that Dunk had received his award, he wasn't about to give up that easily.

He explained that he had now decided to go after the Foreign Office for exemplary damages. The case was based on misfeasance in public office, since exemplary damages had not been covered by the Home Office award. Kormornick thought that the Silcott case might not be insurmountable. In order to succeed, he would have to show that not only had the officials abused their power but they had done so with malice. His courage was admirable, although some could have regarded it as foolhardy.

It had been an excellent lunch and a wonderful celebration. Dunk and I parted as good friends with great hopes for the future, never imagining for a moment that this would be our last meeting.

Kormornick had bet that the Foreign Office would prefer to settle the case and draw a line under the whole unsavoury affair rather than risk any more skeletons being exposed in public. Curiously, Scott had never been able to find out from Egerton just how far up the tree the decision had gone to stop the defence witnesses from coming to court. Luckily for Dunk, this high-risk strategy succeeded. In December 1999, the Foreign Office agreed to pay £125,000 exemplary damages, plus legal costs, to Dunk and Schlesinger. But there was still no admission of liability and no public apology.

Aged eighty, Dunk had dared to take on the might of the state and had won, though he never received the public apology that he was really after. No one had won exemplary damages since 1703, when Judge Holt had fined constables for stopping electors from voting. It was hailed as a heroic victory in the press and was even featured by Sue MacGregor on the *Today Programme*. *The Observer* printed a feature by Nick Cohen titled, "A nod, a wink and a deal. You've been FO'd". That summed it up rather well, I thought.

But by December 1999, events were taking a turn for the worst for Dunk. He was now in poor health and in intensive care. The sixteen-year fight for justice had taken its toll on him. After surviving two heart operations, he was now suffering from cancer. Thankfully, he didn't suffer too much. In February 2000, a great personality was lost to the world. There were obituaries in all of the broadsheets that paid tribute to the man and his long fight for justice against impossible odds.

I telephoned Kormornick for a chat and found him in uncharacteristically low mood.

"Hi, James, have you heard the news about Reg?"

"Yes, I'm so sorry and know what a blow this must be to you after all you've been through together."

"It's so sad and so tragic – all those years wasted and for what?" lamented Kormornick.

"I often wonder whether, after seventeen years, it's worth me holding on any longer in the vain hope that my ship may come in one day. Reg's case is such a cautionary tale. I don't want to end up like him, so should we just forget it?"

"Well, you may be right. But it would be a pity to give up now. Perhaps let's just wait and see. I'm still working on some other cases that might help you. But don't pin all your hopes on it, sorry."

The call ended and I felt more depressed than ever. It all seemed so remote and could be such a colossal waste of time. But what else could I do but hope?

Chapter 24

A Chink of Light

The year 2000 was quite uneventful for me but things were now also looking up for Alex Schlesinger, Dunk's co-defendant. His conviction had been quashed together with Dunk's and the Home Office had also agreed to pay him compensation.

Kormornick had been working on his case also and in October 2010, the *The Guardian* reported that the Home Secretary had awarded him £1.375m plus costs. But there was still nothing for me.

In the months that followed, going into summer 2001, Kormornick was hoping to achieve an important success.

His client, Ali Daghir, of dual Iraqi-British nationality and managing director of Euromac, had been convicted in 1991 and jailed for five years for conspiring to export electrical equipment to Iraq in the so-called 'nuclear triggers' case. He had been caught up in a nineteen-month sting operation conducted by US and UK Customs with the personal approval of Margaret Thatcher. His defence was based on entrapment and that the equipment was not specially designed for use in nuclear weapons.

There was further embarrassment for the government in June 1994, when Lord Taylor quashed the conviction. Judge Denison had misdirected the jury by saying that they could convict if they found that the equipment had any military use. There were other grounds of appeal based on fresh evidence that UN inspectors had found no evidence of Euromac's involvement and that the capacitors were not required in the nuclear project.

But the appeal had succeeded too well; having quashed the conviction based on the misdirection, the other grounds were not heard. This meant that he was not eligible for compensation under the wrongful conviction scheme so he had to fall back on suing Customs for misfeasance in public office and malicious prosecution.

After Ali Daghir had failed to win compensation after a four-week High Court trial in the summer of that year, Kormornick was under some pressure to pull off a prestigious victory. Having spent years slogging away against Customs and putting together what appeared to be a good case based on government documents, it had been a bitter blow to him and his client. Neither was his firm best pleased.

Kormornick tried to bounce back from defeat. He had always believed that the government should have compensated the Matrix Churchill directors. Eventually, he thought, there might be a breakthrough that would take his clients Paul Henderson and Peter Allen into the wrongful charge scheme. If so, this could also be of some value to me.

The ex gratia scheme for wrongful charge was a voluntary scheme operated entirely at the discretion of the Home Secretary. It had existed before the creation of the Court of Criminal Appeal in 1907. Little guidance was offered about the procedure and the criteria.

The whole scheme was veiled in obscurity and decisions were kept secret so it was difficult to navigate around it. The judiciary had been very reluctant to interfere with the Home Secretary's discretion so refusals were difficult, if not impossible, to challenge. The description "Star Chamber" came to mind.

The scheme required a period of time to be spent in custody and serious default by a public body in order to qualify. In the Matrix Churchill case, serious default was not thought to be a difficulty given Scott's helpful findings about serious failures in the disclosure process and the misuse of PII certificates to hide the truth. The real issue was custody. The rules of the scheme had not been defined clearly and there was no reference to any time requirement.

However, in the early part of 2001, two important new facts had emerged. Firstly, apparently once custody was established, there was no minimum time requirement. Secondly, though Henderson and

Allen had been on bail throughout their prosecution, they had spent one night in custody due to an administrative delay in putting their sureties in place.

So, as they had always been on bail, would such a short period in custody suffice, given that technicality? There were no guarantees and, though it was a long shot, it was worth a try since there was nothing to lose.

In November 2001, Kormornick finally received a decision letter from the then Home Secretary, David Blunkett. He opened the envelope nervously, not really knowing what to expect but aware that success would mean so much for Henderson and Allen [and for him] and could also open the door for me. He was at low ebb, bordering on depression and I was seriously concerned about him.

As he raced through the letter to find the decision his heart was beating fast and suddenly he realized that they had succeeded. David Blunkett had accepted that they had satisfied the custody requirement and there had been a serious default by a public authority amounting to a miscarriage of justice and that they were entitled to compensation to be determined by an independent assessor.

The Matrix Churchill case had been very high profile, so the decision was of great interest to the media. It even made the front page of *The Independent*. Most people welcomed the decision, even if it had taken the government nine long years after the spectacular collapse of the case to draw a line "under one of the more unsavoury episodes in Whitehall history", as *The Independent* put it.

I lost no time in calling Kormornick to congratulate him and find out how this could help my own case.

"Hi Lawrence, I've just read about Matrix Churchill. Well done indeed. So how did you manage to pull that one off, you old wizard, you?"

"Thanks James; they deserved it but were lucky to find a loophole because of an administrative delay – others may not be as fortunate."

"So what does this mean for me?"

"Seems that you could apply now because you were in the custody of the court, but it's still a long shot...."

"Okay, that's great. Let's have a go!"

So Kormornick applied on my behalf, as well as for several others, including John Grecian. The third Matrix Churchill director, Trevor Abraham, had also applied through his defence lawyer.

My case was based on having spent four weeks in the custody of the court at trial and a serious default by a public authority. Though I was granted unconditional bail throughout the prosecution when the court was in recess, my bail was suspended during court sessions.

But luck had run out and we were all turned down in 2002 because we had fai.ed to satisfy the custody requirement. It all seemed rather odd and illogical. Perhaps the Treasury had become worried about the potential financial burden on the public purse.

It became apparent that David Blunkett had decided that although Henderson and Allen's case was exceptional, he wasn't prepared to exercise his discretion any further. It must have appeared odd to Abraham to be excluded, given that his co-directors had succeeded. Some may say that this was expedient. But such were the vagaries of government.

There was great disappointment, especially for me, and the timing could not have been worse. The Matrix Churchill success had raised my hopes so much. Worst of all, my financial situation had become worse than dire and the prospect of bankruptcy was now looming.

Chapter 25

On Carey Street

The year 2003 did not get off to a brilliant start for either Kormornick or me.

Life had become impossible – no job, no income, no compensation, along with the liability to pay court costs and income tax. After twenty years of a hand-to-mouth existence, loans from friends and mounting debts, I was quite unable to pay those costs and the tax.

Life also had its difficulties for Kormornick. Having spent ten years building up a specialist practice, his firm had decided that crime did not pay. He had been part of the business fraud unit and legal aid changes meant that the work was no longer profitable for a City firm. This resulted in redundancy. All of his clients except for me decided that it was in their best interests to remain with the firm.

To make matters worse, his mother, Joyce, was suffering from terminal cancer and he was spending most weekends in Manchester caring for her with his sister, Suzanne, and brother-in-law, Michael. They were very close indeed and Joyce was a major influence in his life, totally devoted to her family. She passed away at home in June of that year, greatly mourned and sadly missed by her family and friends. The world had come crashing down around him and I was concerned. During this period, we spent much time together trying to keep our spirits up and we became close friends, a friendship that has become very special to me.

The situation had become desperate for me. I considered the various options left and thought that I should consult the Inland Revenue about my inability to pay. I visited their offices in Euston Road to explain my predicament.

To my surprise, I was met by a most helpful lady who sympathized with my situation. Bankruptcy seemed to be the only solution and she explained the process. Though she had been helpful and understanding, I left the meeting with a certain sense of diffidence and a deep sense of failure.

In the days that followed I thought very carefully about the option of bankruptcy and the consequences. Ordinarily, I would never have imagined such a thing and the stigma attached to it – the final humiliation after all I'd been through. But there was really no other choice and at least this would give me a fresh start.

So I took the decision to declare bankruptcy. There were no assets since all my possessions had been sold in the cause of school fees. I felt bad about the Inland Revenue as they had been helpful and patient. I had not expected to be faced with those litigation costs.

There was a strong element of disgrace and shame about bankruptcy. I had fought hard for what was rightfully mine, and was now being forced into financial leprosy for the next two years. The fact that I could not obtain credit was an inconvenience rather than a hardship, although I could not get a mortgage even if I were able to find a job. But at least I had few commitments and expenses and, thankfully, the last of my four children had finished school.

Several weeks passed and one morning a brown envelope from the court arrived containing the petition for bankruptcy issued by the Inland Revenue. Though it made depressing reading, a sense of resignation had set in. My attention was now focused on a preliminary hearing at the Royal Courts of Justice in order to get the process over with as quickly as possible.

Within the environs of the High Courts of Justice, there is a more modern building, named the Thomas More. This is accessible only through the usual tortuous warren of corridors. In that building resides the Bankruptcy Division of the High Court, which is where I found myself one September morning in 2003.

I registered with the court usher, who politely asked me to wait my turn. It was not long before the green light appeared on the registrar's door and I was ushered into chambers. The lady registrar was very pleasant, and was clearly anxious to help anyone avoid bankruptcy if at all feasible.

"Mr Edmiston, this petition has been made by the Commissioners of Inland Revenue. Is there any way you can pay off a small amount every month?"

"Ma'am, they have been extremely fair with me. I have been to see them at their offices in Euston Road, and have explained the circumstances. They were very helpful."

"Why, then, can you not pay?" she enquired.

"I was meeting the commitment, and then my efforts to pull in fees from barristers proved only partially successful. The court costs were becoming astronomical, so as a last resort I sued the head of the chambers with whom I had made the original contract on behalf of his tenant barristers. I also sued the chambers' solicitors who failed to obtain these payments and had recommended that I should pursue them to the end. It was an attempt to retrieve what was rightfully mine from all the drawn-out litigation. This was unsuccessful, hence the £60,000 bill."

"Why did you attempt it?"

"Ma'am, you see, I felt I had to pay the debt to the Inland Revenue, and having used all my assets to pay school fees, there was nothing left to sell. This was my only course. I really have tried. Now, obviously, I'm no longer in chambers."

The registrar paused before making a decision. It all seemed so inevitable.

"Very well, Mr Edmiston, I will make the order. Within a week, you must make an appointment with the Official Receiver at the offices in Bloomsbury. They will ask you for a statement of all your possessions and earnings."

"Thank you, Ma'am."

"I'm sorry it has to be this way because it's clear to me that you really have made every effort. Good luck to you."

And so the bankruptcy order was made on 3 September 2003. This was the last straw after all my efforts over some twenty years to keep my head above water.

I duly made the appointment with, and then visited, the Official Receiver. I went through my bank statements and insurance policies, and was given various instructions as to what I could and could not do. Credit cards were clearly off the menu (I am all the happier for never having had a credit card since). I had to inform my banks of my new status, or at the lack thereof.

There was no problem except with my account at HSBC in Fleet Street. I received a curt, pompous letter from the manager to the effect that the bank did not entertain bankrupts as customers in any way whatsoever. This was upsetting and I felt a trifle insulted.

The bank, however, did retain the positive balance of £54.00, and ignored two letters of my protestations. I was acutely embarrassed by the whole business and eventually was extremely relieved to be formally discharged from bankruptcy on April Fool's Day 2005.

In the months that followed after bankruptcy, efforts were made to find work. I had applied for about 100 different jobs. Some did reach the interview stage, although the most commonly employed rationale for refusal was that of advancing years and over-qualification.

From these applications, the greatest disappointment by far was not being selected for a management job in St Helena, a volcanic island of 10 by 5 miles, with a population of 5,000. The position had been advertised in *The Times*, and seclusion from society, hidden in the traditional gubernatorial residence in Jamestown, rather appealed.

The only form of transport to get to Britain's second oldest colony (after Bermuda) was by RMS *St Helena* from Cape Town, the voyage taking some seven days to complete. There are roads there, and it was recommended that the successful candidate's car be fitted with special front brakes, and plenty of spare pads to be taken out, since the roads are so steep.

Obviously the main problem with the place was, apart from the wild mid-Atlantic environment, a complete lack of airport. Crack that one and the place would have been stiff with package tourists from France seeing where Napoleon Bonaparte spent his final days. And, of course, there would have been the usual quests to establish whether or not the perfidious English had poisoned him in 1821.

There might have been some interest from South African tourists, especially Zulus, whose King Cetshwayo had dealt the British Army a good hiding in 1879 at Isandlwana, as he too was parked there out of harm's way. Further enemies that had been confined to the island in their time were Afrikaner prisoners of war. Stuck there, there was absolutely no hope of escaping and rejoining a Boer Kommando.

Other positions of interest that received some sort of reaction were: a bursar at an Oxford college; managing a theatrical costumier; secretaryship of a prestigious fishing club; and running an employment agency supplying African staff to the catering trade whose adherence to the immigration laws, however, sounded decidedly suspect.

The position of curator of the Lords Cricket Museum was also advertised. I had been at Brasenose College with Stephen Green (with the unmistakable initials S.E.A.) who had decided to retire. Being well acquainted with that fascinating museum, I knew that Green had done a really fine job.

I dashed off an application form, only to receive the usual "thanks, but no thanks" letter. At a college dinner some time later, I saw Green and came clean that I had applied to the MCC for that job. Green laughed and admitted that if he had had to apply at that time there was no way that even he would have landed the position. Apparently, they had been turning down retired generals, admirals and academics of note. The competition was quite awesome.

"But Jim, I do wish you'd told me that you were applying," Green said wistfully. By then, I had had my confidence beaten out of me to such an extent that I could not have brought myself to use any contacts whatsoever for fear of letting them down.

It was at this time an opportunity arose to make a non-polluting car exhaust system. In the last two years of my ownership of Sterling, John Wright Bailey, a former motorcycle champion, had approached me. He had won the German motorcycle and sidecar grand prix in 1975; but that was not his only achievement there. He had actually constructed five bike rigs of his own, and this success was won in competition with the Japanese and the mighty BMW works organization.

This appealed to my belief in all things concerning British engineering. We joined together, and having created history by securing two successive development grants from the Department of Trade and Industry, a Sterling motorcycle, based on the former racing bikes, was born.

This prototype, which was able to be ridden, sported a 500cc four-cylinder horizontally opposed two-stroke engine that achieved 96bhp. Brakes and instruments had to be imported from Italy and Japan, but the rest was British.

When Sterling was sold, the new owners demanded to keep the project as part of the sale as it had been a purely Sterling investment in their eyes. Coincidentally, when a neighbour of Bailey's, who was a secretary at the Japanese Trade Mission, overheard that a motorcycle project was being offered for sale to the Japanese, an incandescent Bailey drove straight round to Sterling and removed the whole lot on the back of a lorry. The project died there and then.

Bailey, working on his own, had some success in a water purification invention. However, his patents were stolen from him outrageously by one of the large water companies.

Later, he got back in touch with me to see if we could work on something together. At my instigation, Bailey came up with an exhaust system derived from his water purification ideas that cleaned up vehicle emissions without using a catalytic converter.

The readings from the independent tests carried out at Ford's Dunton Centre were astounding for the Aerated Column Reactor. A more spectacular demonstration was often given by Bailey holding a white handkerchief over the exhaust tail pipe while the vehicle ran for thirty minutes or more. The handkerchief became damp but in no way sooty or discoloured. Every 5,000 miles, a sludge collector could be emptied and the contents disposed of.

I paid for the prototypes, and to patent part of the intellectual property. We both reckoned that if we disclosed all the information in order to obtain a full patent, someone with proper resources would design around it and might improve it. Then the prime objective of the new exhaust systems moved because of legislation to concentrate on the reduction of carbon dioxide emission, which is not noxious in itself.

As it stood, the ACR reduced CO_2 emission by nearly forty per cent. This was not good enough for Bailey, the perfectionist. Not accepting anything less than 100 per cent of CO_2 emission being eliminated, he knew that it could be achieved, and so development continued.

There followed approaches from various potential investors both at home and overseas. The problem was one of trust. Bailey was just not prepared to risk losing any control whatsoever of the project in its development to perfection.

At this time, I had the good fortune to be helped by two very close Oxford friends; John Olsen, who had been the commercial director of Cathay Pacific Airways, and Bill Hadman, a graduate also of Harvard Business School. Bill, who had established a paint factory for British Paints in Bangalore, gave me an introduction to the Tata Empire. I made an outline presentation to Tata Motors, who, before their acquisition of Jaguar Land Rover from the Ford Motor Company, maintained a body of some eighty development engineers at Warwick University, and they signed a preliminary confidentiality agreement.

But there was a new problem; Bailey had died very suddenly and unexpectedly. His widow was even more determined that nobody would benefit from Bailey's labour without a complete up-front buyout. Whilst understandable, this was just not practical, especially as the development had not been quite finished. The couple had had a tough life financially and had lost something so valuable in the past that she was just not prepared for any element of risk ever again.

And so the ACR project died in an insoluble impasse. But while Bailey was alive, it provided me with an interesting and encouraging prospect, and the possibility of a ladder out of poverty.

Chapter 26

Enough Time in Court?

Although 2003 had hardly been a vintage year for Kormornick and me, things were starting to improve a little.

While I was busy dealing with the bankruptcy, and trying to stave off my creditors and survive, Kormornick was also trying to get back on his feet again. Having joined the partnership of a two-partner West End firm off Marylebone High Street, he had lost no time in continuing his efforts for me and the prospect of some compensation was looking better. There were some encouraging signs from other similar cases.

Trevor Abraham and John Grecian were not content to accept the refusal to admit them into the government scheme. They were in the process of preparing a judicial review to challenge the refusal.

The basis of the challenge was that once the custody condition was established, there was no minimum time requirement and that "custody" included any time spent in the custody of the court. It had seemed a bit odd that Abraham had not been treated in the same way as his co-directors. These two test cases were the strongest and the advice was for me to await the outcome before taking any further steps.

Judicial review is a quaint and often uncertain procedure whereby a public body can be challenged over an unreasonable administrative decision. The test of unreasonableness is a high threshold to cross. Under Lord Diplock's classification, a decision is unreasonable if it is "so outrageous in its defiance of logic or of accepted moral standards that no sensible person who had applied his mind to the question could have arrived at it." So in order to quash the decision, the applicants would have to show whether any home secretary acting reasonably would have come to such a decision – not an easy task by any stretch of the imagination.

The judicial review eventually came before Mr Justice Henriques at the end of 2004. The case was hard fought by both sides and there was much at stake for all concerned. Ed Fitzgerald QC and Nick Bowen represented the applicants and presented a very cogent submission. They performed superbly in an extremely difficult case, with limited funding. The stakes were high for Grecian, Abraham and me. A liberal interpretation of the custody criterion could lead to an increase in eligibility, especially businessmen like me with substantial claims. If so, this would not be welcomed by the Treasury.

It had been a long wait for Abraham and Grecian and they were not getting any younger either. On 3 December 2004, it was time for Mr Justice Henriques to publish his judgment. There had been no indication whatever of the way it was likely to go and judicial review is often a long shot.

But as it turned out, there was a ray of hope for us. The decision was quashed and the case sent back to the Home Secretary, David Blunkett. The following passage of the judgment was of particular relevance to me:

> I adopt the helpful approach of Mr Bowen … that a reasonable and literate man would conclude that a "period in custody" is any occasion when someone is not free to leave the court or the police station at a time of his own choosing.

So, after twenty-one years, the way was now clear for me to reapply to the Home Office based on this decision. Kormornick was looking forward to telephoning me with the good news.

"James, I've got some joy for you!"

"I could do with that after being made bankrupt. It's been pretty dire lately."

"The judicial review was successful and, more importantly for you, the judge has said that being in the custody of the court falls within the custody requirement of the scheme. So you should now be able to satisfy that requirement."

"Fantastic news! I just can't believe it after all these years. So what's next?"

"Well, though it's looking more positive, it may still take some time yet. We need to file a resubmission as soon as possible just in case the government makes any changes to the scheme to tighten or even abolish it."

"You're joking, aren't you? Do you really think they'd do that now?"

"Yes; it wouldn't surprise me at all. They won't welcome this decision on custody. And if they did make any changes, it would stuff your claim well and truly."

"Oh my God! You'd better get this filed as soon as possible. I can't believe that having got this far I could still end up with nothing. What more do I have to do?"

"Okay, James, I understand only too well and have been working on this case for eight years myself. I'll get the resubmission filed immediately. There should still be time but I was planning to go away for Christmas."

"What? But you don't celebrate Christmas, do you?"

"Heard of multiculturalism?

"Thanks a bunch Lawrence," said I, still doubtful as ever.

Chapter 27

Hope Springs Eternal

Christmas 2004 was now approaching and the various office parties lit up the West End, but not for Edmiston. Thankfully, Kormornick was not too distracted by all the festivities in Marylebone and he was true to his word to file the papers promptly.

The resubmission was duly filed on 21 December, in good time for the holiday season and while the scheme remained live. Given that the miscarriage of justice had taken place some twenty years earlier, Kormornick had also asked for the resubmission to be expedited. After all, the Home Office had caused a delay by wrongly deciding that I had not satisfied the custody criterion. But it was still in the lap of the gods. And there was little that could be done to expedite the resubmission short of applying to the court in the event of excessive delay, which was not really a practical option.

With the papers filed, Kormornick and I met for a pre-Christmas drink in Marylebone High Street, and to review the coming year and anticipate what hope that might bring.

Marylebone High Street used to be one of the most boring thoroughfares in all London. The shops comprised the usual chemist, grocer, butcher and fishmonger interspersed with the odd patisserie, building society and newsagent. Such outfits as ironmonger, draper, dry-salter and haberdasher had once existed.

These roles have now been filled by the stereotypical multi-nationals in other parts of the city. Amazingly, apothecaries had long since gone. There was also the usual selection of charity shops. In short, the street catered for staid local London residents whose most exciting purchase would have been nothing more than knicker elastic.

Today, Marylebone High Street abounds with boutiques, art galleries, antiquarian bookshops, gastronomic restaurants, epicurean specialist delicatessens and all manner of unique and interesting emporia. The locals hold a street fair every year. There is a Sunday market where the produce is unparalleled, partially due to the exigencies of a strong smart clientele of pouting Parisian *mesdames* and their nubile teenage daughters. It even vies with Bond Street and Knightsbridge for sheer chic and retail quality.

The two of us sat down in a local wine bar. We talked while subconsciously surveying the cosmopolitan passers-by, reminiscing over the past and how all could now change for me. But it still seemed too much to hope for. Things were definitely looking up but there were still hurdles to overcome. The scheme was discretionary. Even if the custody requirement was satisfied, there was still the serious default condition to meet.

That said, the interference by senior public officials with the witnesses was, arguably, as bad as it gets. Nevertheless, Kormornick, though cautiously optimistic, advised me not to assume anything. And I would have to wait another nine months or more for a decision, so there would be still more nail-biting to come.

That Christmas and New Year was a happier time for me and my family as they eagerly awaited the outcome of my resubmission. At least now there was hope. It had been a tough year for Kormornick, who took the opportunity of a last-minute holiday to the Alps for himself and his family. He needed the fresh mountain air and some exercise to clear his mind and recharge his batteries ready for the challenges of the coming year.

As with all holidays, the festive break passed by very speedily and Kormornick quickly found himself back at work. Inevitably there were the endless requests from me for an update. Sadly, there was nothing to report in January. Kormornick was keen not to press the Home Office too much at such an early stage and risk alienating the case officer.

Eventually, a letter from the Home Office arrived in the middle of February acknowledging receipt of the resubmission. The case worker, though sympathetic and helpful, was unable to provide a timescale for a substantive response. The Miscarriage of Justice team at the Home Office were always polite and helpful.

It was disappointing to be left in a black hole. After twenty-one years, I was keen to get on with my life, finally. Kormornick was still concerned not to press the Home Office but was prevailed upon to at least speak with the case officer in order to try to get some idea of timescales.

Thankfully, she seemed quite receptive to his gentle probing and polite enquiry. Though it was some consolation to discover that the resubmission was being considered on an expedited basis, sadly it was still not possible to provide a timescale for a substantive response. Naturally, I was all impatient but would just have to wait another few months for yet another update.

Spring arrived and hope sprang eternal, as they say. I pestered Kormornick to give another gentle reminder, so he telephoned for an update. The conversation went very well.

"Good morning, I'm really sorry to bother you again but is there any news I can give my long-suffering client, please?"

"Good morning, Mr Kormornick, I'm afraid that I'm still unable to provide a timescale, though I'm now able to give you a response about the custody criterion."

"That would be really helpful please."

"It has now been decided that in the light of the judgment on Grecian and Abraham, it is accepted that Mr Edmiston meets the custody criterion and we are now in the process of considering the other criteria under the ex gratia scheme."

"Thank you for that indication; I'm sure Mr Edmiston will be pleased to learn that. So we'll now just have to wait a little while longer for the final decision."

Kormornick telephoned me immediately.

"James, I've just spoken with the Home Office and there seems to be some good news for you at last."

"Oh really? What's that? Do we finally have a timescale or am I going to end up waiting longer than Josef K to discover my fate?"

"Well, hopefully not … and we still don't have a timescale, but they have made a decision on whether you satisfy the custody criterion."

"Really? What?"

"You're in!"

"What?"

"You're in! You satisfy the custody requirement! So that just leaves the remaining criterion of serious default."

"Lawrence, that's fantastic news! I just can't believe it. Thanks so much."

"Yes, it's great news and I'm delighted for you."

"Do you have it in writing?"

"No, but don't worry, I'll be writing to them today to confirm it."

"So dare I now ask about the chances of success on serious default?"

"Well, it should be okay. Frankly, given the findings of the Scott Report, it would be difficult to imagine how the Home Office could possibly conclude that this did not amount to serious default. But stranger things have happened."

"Okay, you bloody lawyers can never guarantee anything," I sneered. "It's always on the one hand or on the other!"

"True, so you'd better try to find a one-armed lawyer," joked Kormornick, fully aware how frustrating lawyers can be with their endless equivocations and caveats.

Chapter 28

Success but no Apology

The months passed by slowly in 2005 awaiting the final decision from the Home Office.

I even wondered if having a new Home Secretary might make a difference. At the end of 2004, there had been some damaging revelations about David Blunkett's private life. As usual, the media had a field day. Apparently, a visa application for his ex-lover's nanny had been fast-tracked so he felt that resignation was right and proper. Ironically, there certainly had not been any fast-tracking in my case. Downing Street named the Education Secretary, Charles Clarke, as Blunkett's replacement.

Clarke was soon at the centre of attention for his proposals for countering terrorism. Critics had suggested that his reforms to the judicial system had undermined centuries of British legal precedent dating back to the Magna Carta, particularly the right to a fair trial and trial by jury. He was also criticized for continuing to push through the Identity Cards Bill. This was seen by some as a serious infringement of privacy, but Clarke considered it necessary to combat terrorism. So I was concerned that he might not be over sympathetic to my cause.

Eventually, in October 2005, an envelope arrived from the Home Office with the decision letter. Kormornick reflected back to happier times four years earlier in 2001, when Henderson and Allen had succeeded. They had indeed been quite fortunate, but much had changed. Would I be so lucky?

As he removed the letter in nervous expectation, Kormornick

raced over the text eager to find out his client's fate. The second paragraph of the letter read:

> After careful consideration of the relevant circumstances, the Home Secretary has decided to make, without admission of liability, a payment of compensation to Mr Edmiston under the provisions of the ex-gratia scheme....

So there was success at last. Kormornick couldn't quite believe it. He had always been worried that the government would try to find some way to weasel out of it. But Clarke had, in fact, done the decent thing by accepting that there was a serious default by a public authority amounting to a miscarriage of justice and that I was entitled to compensation. An apology also would have been welcomed but that was not Home Office policy. Kormornick felt a huge sense of relief and excitement at the thought of calling his long-term client with the glad tidings.

"James, are you sitting comfortably?"

"Oh no, not you again! What is it now?"

"That's no way to speak to someone who has just persuaded the government to compensate you."

"You ... what? Not another of your funnies?"

"Well, not quite. But if you don't believe me, just come down to the office and see it in black and white."

"I'm on my way...."

I trotted down Paddington Street and was soon sitting in the subterranean waiting room of Kormornick's offices on Weymouth Street. He rushed down to greet me clutching the letter, which he thrust before my very eyes, insisting, "There it is, ye of little faith, see for yourself."

I couldn't quite take in the contents of the letter. After twenty-two years of struggle, this letter could now change the course of my life. Having just turned sixty-two, this was a most welcome birthday gift. A warm hue of exhilaration radiated within me. Kormornick snapped me from this reverie to usher me out of the office to celebrate.

A most enjoyable lunch ensued with much humour and reflection. At long last, there was some time for some prandial relaxation. Coming to terms with all the events of the last twenty-two years was still not easy after so many ups and downs. I was also delighted for Kormornick that he had been able to pull off this miracle for me. It gave him a great sense of pride and personal satisfaction.

It was quite incredible to think that success had finally arrived, but little did I know that the back-breaking work on assessment was about to begin and would be drawn out another three long years. For now, at least, I could relax a little to enjoy Christmas and New Year with my family, hoping that the future was brighter.

The path of compensation never runs true. There were some heart-stopping moments in 2006. In April, Charles Clarke suddenly closed down the ex gratia scheme with immediate effect. Victims of miscarriage of justice and their trusted lawyers were up in arms in the absence of any prior consultation.

Clarke put forward a most curious case. He argued that the compensation scheme had become too expensive to administer, was costing the taxpayer £2 million per annum, and that the focus should be on the victims of crime. Others argued, however, that he'd miscalculated. The actual saving was less than the annual cost of cleaning out the bins at the House of Commons.

The absence of any consultation or prior warning of the abolition of the scheme was considered by many as unlawful. The decision effectively meant that many victims of miscarriage of justice would have no remedy for wrongful charge or conviction.

So I had got in by the skin of my teeth. Kormornick had been right yet again to lose no time whatever in filing the resubmission. It was chilling to think that I could have been shut out by Clarke. Others, whose applications had not been filed on time, were not so lucky. Though their protests reached the Court of Appeal, sadly, their pleas fell on deaf ears and they were to remain uncompensated.

Chapter 29

Another Long Battle

A very pleasant Christmas and New Year celebrating the success with my family was soon followed by the very welcome first interim payment of the Home Office Compensation Scheme, which arrived in early 2006. The £50,000 cheque helped to relieve the more dire vicissitudes of my existence. But now I was back to face some serious work.

There was always some drama for me. The cheque was walked around to the nearest HSBC and duly banked. Consequently, I issued some of my own cheques to pay bills, including legal fees. As luck would have it, the cheque to the lawyers bounced because the bank teller had recorded the credit as £5,000, only, one assumes, in error. The matter was finally sorted out after ten days of arguing and without any apology whatsoever on the part of HSBC ('the local bank').

There now had to be a strategy laid down for the preparation and submission of the claim for assessment. I had never dared to dream of success and had little idea of the daunting task that lay ahead. Kormornick had so far shielded me from the rigours of the assessment process and did not quite know how to break the news without causing further distress.

The compensation process had already exhausted Reg Dunk, who had died within a year of his award. I was now sixty-two and young Kormornick was acutely aware that the process could take a similar toll on my health (and, perhaps, his). So he thought that the best thing to do would be to talk me through the process over a coffee. He broke the unwelcome news gently at Starbucks, Marylebone High Street, around the corner from where I was living.

There was definitely a renewed spring in my step.

"Hi, Lawrence, so good to see you. How are you?"

"Well, thanks, James. Good to see you looking so well."

"Absolutely. It's the thought of all that compensation that you're going to get for me and sorting my life out. And of course I want to do the right thing by Sisi and the kids, who have also suffered so much. Pity the scheme doesn't include an apology; that's also really important to us."

We got some coffee and found a quiet corner to chat.

Many things were going through my mind and I was anxious to know more about compensation and the timescale.

"So how much am I likely to get for twenty-three years to clear my name?" I wondered.

"Well, there's compensation for pain and suffering and for financial loss but it's not easy to say how much until we have more details," was the qualified response.

Bloody lawyers, I thought. Why are they so incapable of giving a straight answer to a simple question, and why does everything have to be so complicated and take so long?

I bit my lip and thought some gentle probing might work better.

"Okay, then, but how much approximately for twenty-three years' pain and suffering? Surely that must run into hundreds of thousands of pounds alone?

"Well, not exactly, James...."

"What?"

"Yes, okay, it's complicated. But basically, you didn't go to prison and have made a fairly good recovery, and the future is looking brighter."

"So?"

"So, we're probably talking about £75,000 absolute maximum based on the personal injury scale."

"What? That's outrageous! You're having me on, aren't you? Is this another one of your pathetic little jokes...?"

"Look, James, I can understand your disappointment but you have to bear in mind that victims of serious miscarriages who have spent years in prison in appalling conditions may not even get more than, say, £300,000 for pain and suffering. Seems that the going rate is about £14,000 per year spent in prison, so your award has to fall below that, I'm afraid."

"Is that all? That can't be right. What about damage to reputation?"

"Yes, you're right, but again, not a lot. Pity you weren't a rock star or a footballer ... they get more ... but it's not all doom and gloom really."

"Oh, really? Doesn't sound very promising to me!"

"Hopefully, given what you've told me about business loss, providing you can back it up, you may get a total award somewhere in the region of Reg's, all being well, but who knows with the new Assessor?"

"Okay, it's beginning to sound a little better, even if it's all subject to your usual qualifications. This depends, that depends ... very tedious really. And how long is this whole bloody thing now likely to take? Another twenty-three years?"

"Well, it could take certainly another three years or more," Kormornick hesitated, anxious not to draw further aspersions on the legal profession.

"What! You mean after waiting twenty-three years, I'm now going to have to wait until I'm sixty-five or older? Why does it all take so long?"

Kormornick then explained about the mammoth paperwork task that was required going back as far as the 1970s.

"That's bloody unfair! How can they expect me to provide all this after twenty-three years? It seems that no matter what we do, there's always another impossible hurdle to try to prevent me from being properly compensated. Perhaps they're hoping that I'll croak first, like Reg."

"It is most unfair," said Kormornick with sympathy. "But what can we do except try to work through it and do our best, I suppose? Poor Reg had a similar problem, I'm afraid. To make matters worse, the paperwork task in your case is much harder, stretching back as far as 1972. And frankly, I'm not even sure what documents will still be around after this length of time. However, let's see what the accounting expert says."

"Then what about another interim payment, or do they intend to leave me like this for the next three years or longer?"

"I'll see what can be done but it's discretionary and it could take another six months or so."

This certainly dampened down my spirits. Collating so much historic paperwork would be daunting, to say the least, and I desperately needed another interim payment soon just to live and to clear off some more long overdue debts. The conversation then turned to who would make my assessment. Kormornick explained about the clandestine scheme and the Independent Assessor, Lord Brennan QC.

In 2001, Lord Brennan QC had succeeded Sir David Calcutt QC, who had made the assessments for Dunk and Schlesinger totalling some £4 million. The word on the street was that there were to be no more "Dunks" and that Lord Brennan was an absolute stickler for detail. So all the facts had to be included and each one had to be backed up by witness statements and hard documentary evidence together with a detailed report from an accounting expert. The Home Secretary had appointed the Assessor and there was no right to an oral hearing so my case would be decided on paper behind closed doors. Judicial review was the only appeal but this was virtually impossible.

By this time my head was spinning and I felt a bad headache coming on. As usual, I was desperate for some money and simply could not believe how much time and effort would still be required. Another three years or more to reach a final award seemed enormously futuristic. Where would I find all these documents?

Much of the past had been put to the back of my mind in order to try to move forward. The thought of having to dredge all this up again was terrifying. The real problem was that my family would also be put through the distress and inconvenience of having to give exhaustive witness statements going into intimate detail. The whole thing would be degrading and humiliating in the extreme.

I returned home to reflect on the enormity of the task, whom to approach, how I could gather the information and any documents that might still be available. There was one good thing: the book I had published in 1992 about my time at Sterling, the Customs case and the consequences – *The Sterling Years*. Thankfully, it was an extremely useful contemporaneous record, which could now be used to refresh my memory for the compensation case.

Gathering documents would be far more difficult. I had retained some of my papers. Living a quasi-nomadic life, many of these, by dint of sheer weight, had been disposed of over the years. Law firms usually keep documents for only twelve years at most. It was unlikely that Payne Hicks Beach would have any left.

There was another possibility. Those who had been closely associated with me during this period might be able to add some credence by giving witness statements. However, there arose the task of tracking them down and establishing whether or not they would be able to help me. In my reduced circumstances, I had hardly been the hub of social activity about town and had lost touch. It was a question of with whom to start and how to find them.

The next week was spent trying to locate people and documents. For the next few months I took on the role of investigator extraordinaire, if I do say so myself. My first task was to telephone Payne Hicks Beach, my former solicitors in New Square in Lincoln's Inn. I knew Anthony Slingsby's address, but he and John Manuell had long since left. Locating Manuell and finding any papers that might have still been around was vital. An appointment was made to meet Guy Green, the current managing partner, and enquiries were made about Manuell. Perhaps the firm would know of his whereabouts either in England or Australia, if he had gone back home. There was no forwarding address. One of the secretaries seemed to remember that he had left to take up an appointment with Messrs Lipkin Gorman & Co in London.

I immediately telephoned that law firm. The disappointing response was that he had left some seven years earlier, again with no forwarding address. But on further enquiry, it seemed that Manuell had gone in the direction of immigration law. With little else to go on,

I searched the current Butterworth's Law Directory, but to no avail. His name was listed as neither a barrister nor a solicitor. How strange; had a man of such talent abandoned the law after all this time?

Kormornick was told of my singular lack of success. He dipped into the arcane world of immigration law and who-was-who therein. Lo and behold, like extracting the magician's white rabbit from the top hat, Manuell had reappeared as an immigration judge. But would a judge be prepared to help me given his position? And how much could he recall twenty years on?

Thoughts turned to whether David Howroyd, Sterling's former works director, could help. But he had become unwell. Kormornick and I went to visit him in his home in Dagenham. En route we passed the old Sterling factory. It was very nostalgic to reflect back on it all. Kormornick, as usual, had a thousand questions to ask me but I was just lost in thought and he took the hint.

I mused that, when one thinks of Dagenham, political associations do not usually come to mind. Whereas it is generally remembered as an industrial area in Essex, where the Ford car plant was once based in our industrial heyday, it actually does have political associations, through Sterling, and the time in 1968 when female workers walked out in protest against sexual discrimination, which eventually led to the Equal Pay Act.

When we arrived at Howroyd's house the reception was cordial but the atmosphere was a little tense, with his wife Dorothy in the background. Understandably, Howroyd was hesitant to become involved in anything that might dig up the past and disturb his hard-earned, though modest, retirement. Bitter memories of the Customs interview, the trial and the sad demise of Sterling had remained with him over the years. He was also worried about doing anything that would bring him face-to-face with the authorities again, so, sadly, there would be no compensation for him.

He had his own theory of what was behind the thoughts of Her Majesty's Government. They were essentially desirous of killing off the private arms companies like Sterling. Ultimately, they managed to secure Sterling and Enfield together under the mantle of British Aerospace, which had assumed control over the Royal Ordnance Factories.

The government knew that Sterling, being a privately owned company, could not withstand any long court battles as its financial resources were obviously limited. It was making "sharp" goods complete, and was probably one of the smaller of the defence manufacturers. How cheap and convenient it was for the government to make an example to be seen to be doing "the right thing".

When Howroyd wrote his excellent book, *The Guns of Dagenham*, with Peter Laidler, he discovered that all the recent firearms registers that were taken from Sterling were mysteriously unavailable. This may or may not connect with the fact that the British Government might have made a serious error of judgement by selling Heckler & Koch small arms of German manufacture through the conduit of RSAF Enfield to the Middle East, including nations contiguous with Israel, with all its American sensitivities. Who knows?

Keith Cole, Sterling's accountant, would have been a most useful asset, but he had disappeared. Considerable time was spent looking for him, but I could turn up no trace whatsoever. We had last met when I had been working in chambers. He had visited me out of the blue to request a character reference. He was contemplating taking holy orders in the Church of England. I duly wrote the letter, without even bordering on perjury. I also checked with the Church, but no dog-collared Cole was as yet spreading widely God's word. Perhaps one day he will re-emerge.

Kormornick had told me that evidence from Sterling's accountants in the early 1980s would be helpful. Tim Chessells had left and gone on to prove himself as quite an outstanding businessman. He went on to be knighted in 1993 for his success in running the North East Thames Regional Health Authority. Sir Tim had then gone on to be Chairman of the British Telecom Pension Scheme trustees, and Hermes Pension Management. At one time, he had been Chairman of the Legal Aid Board. He was a keen shooting man and could clearly remember my tribulations at Sterling: of course, he was prepared to help, if he could, but he needed to refresh his memory with the papers from the time.

The next person to contact was Stephen Adamson. He had been the corporate recovery partner at Arthur Young McClelland Moores

& Co. He had advised the bank about Sterling in 1983 and was prepared to help if he could, but he also needed to refresh his memory with the papers from the time.

Locating any Sterling papers was paramount. Kormornick and I arranged to meet with Guy Green, now the senior partner of Payne Hicks Beach. Green had been at Oxford, but had originally met me in the confines of University College London law library, where we both had permission to work during vacations.

Green said that he would do everything he could to help. He thought that the likelihood of actually finding any useful papers was remote. Due to the exorbitant cost of space in the vicinity, a seven-year maximum for the storage of archives was operated before they were systematically destroyed. He did actually find a few papers, but they were all that remained and not that helpful.

Kormornick took the opportunity of visiting Green once more, in his inimitable terrier-like manner. He pleaded to be taken down to the archive cellars, where he was left for some time to satisfy his forlorn enquiry. The cellars would have been put to much better use, he thought, with orderly racks of vintage port and claret.

It was just as well that the rest of the Payne Hicks Beach partners had not thought along those lines, although Slingsby had been big in the Law Society wine circle, for Kormornick suddenly spotted something. He had stumbled across a large cardboard storage box of files marked "Edmiston". He then caught sight of another "Edmiston" storage box. In all, five such crates dating back over twenty-five years were hauled from that subterranean dungeon. Kormornick was like the curiously-named Spaniard, Ponce de Leon, on the realization of his quest for the Fountain of Youth.

I trawled the Bank of Scotland, but retirement to distant parts, and death, had overtaken those who could have been of use. The Oxford Street branch had long been closed down. I was told that any personal effects would have been taken to the Haymarket branch but that there was nothing there for me either.

Following Kormornick's example, I dropped into the Haymarket branch late one afternoon. I was fully expecting to find a huge sealed parcel of Sterling sub-machine gun drawings deposited with the bank in the early days of my *regnum* at Dagenham, in case the originals might have been destroyed in a factory fire, and there were some papers there. I was unlucky with the drawings, but the bank did reluctantly disgorge some insurance policy documents and two Krugerrands, so my effort was not entirely unrewarded.

Manuell was now an immigration judge sitting in Surbiton. The Immigration Office was based in Croydon at Lunar House (or Loony House, as it was known locally because of its habitual administrative delays).

The ravages of time had not marked Manuell one iota. Our eventual meeting in Surbiton was as if the events of the Old Bailey had taken place a mere two months ago, rather than over twenty years earlier. He remembered me and the case quite well and was prepared to assist where he could, providing he was able to refresh his memory from the files.

He listened intently to my tale of woe and couldn't believe that I had waited twenty-three years for compensation and that Kormornick had found a loophole by pure chance. It was a huge relief that he was prepared to provide a witness statement and, fortunately, the correspondence files were still available to assist him.

So by Christmas 2006, Kormornick had obtained some forty pages of witness statements from Manuell and Slingsby. Their statements, and those of Chessells and Adamson, were of the greatest importance and assistance to Kormornick and me in presenting my case before the Assessor.

It was about this time that I managed to persuade Kormornick to leave the West End to work on my case at his home in Chiswick full-time with The Secretary. In hindsight, this was a wise move because it needed undivided attention.

As we were immersed in this frantic activity into the Edmiston and Sterling archive, I happened to notice the obituary of Egerton in the national press in September, and actually felt a tinge of remorse, ironically. Although his questioning in the Scott Inquiry was to prove to be the very cornerstone of what befell both my past and my future, here was a cultured man whose very raison d'être was at one with my own.

He was one of those British Arabists who fostered the excellent traditional relationship that existed between the Foreign Office and the Arab world in general, before all that was sullied by the misguided ventures of our more recent politicians. He was also commercial in that he actively pushed the cause of UK Plc without letting his standing as a diplomat put him on a pedestal above such mundane minutiae.

So he was just unlucky to be a decent man in the wrong place at the wrong time. Who knows what he knew about the witnesses and whether had he been aware that he might have tried to put a stop to it? Perhaps this may have been concealed from him? We are never likely to find out. But hopefully, after a lifetime of dedicated public service, he will not just be remembered for his appearance before Scott and the rather unfortunate understatement, "Bad show".

But on a lighter note, the *Telegraph* obituary recounted a rather amusing story of a meeting between Saddam and Egerton's 15-year-old son when Saddam had said to him: "Ha, well, grown-up boy. I suppose you've come back to join my army to fight the Kurds?"

His son's face fell a million miles and Saddam laughed – a peculiar sense of humour indeed!

In order to take an overview, it was decided to see counsel, John Tonna, of 39 Essex Street Chambers, in early 2007. Kormornick had worked with him for more than fifteen years and they were also good friends. Here I was, back at my old stamping ground in the Temple area. Dunk's barrister, Peter Irvin, was completely immersed in a long-running case. As I walked past Temple Church, now immortalized by Dan Brown in *The Da Vinci Code*, I reckoned that there had been more suspense and excitement in my own case than in any book of Dan Brown's!

Number 39 Essex Street Chambers were a very smart set opposite the Law Courts. John Tonna, a product of Exeter College Oxford, was a most personable and warm individual, unstuffy, quite different from so many barristers whom I had met in the past. He was also possessed of an amazing intellect and sound judgment.

In the course of the conference, it became apparent that it would be vital to establish the start date for the claim. Though arrests had taken place in February and April 1983, charges had not followed until April 1984, after Sterling had been sold. If the start date was April 1984, the date of wrongful charge, and after the sale of Sterling, that would be a disaster for me. That would prevent me from claiming substantial losses arising from the sale.

After the conference, Kormornick and I went for a drink in the Temple for some post-conference reflection on the start date for the claim, the latest potential crisis. But for me, the poor idiot who had endured a roller-coaster existence these last twenty-three years, it was just another minefield to be avoided.

The dilemma was whether to raise it now or leave it to chance in the final submission. There seemed little point spending a huge amount of time and effort preparing the case on business loss if the start date was uncertain. In the end, it was decided to take a chance and raise it now with the Assessor in order to save time and cost.

Kormornick worked hard on the submission, which was sent to the Assessor in February 2007. The submission relied on the approach the Assessor had adopted in similar cases and that the sale of Sterling had arisen as a direct result of the arrests in 1983. Thankfully, Kormornick had accumulated a vast wealth of knowledge of a scheme operated behind closed doors.

Fortunately for me, my fingernails having already been depleted, it was only necessary to wait a month for a response. Thankfully, the decision of the Assessor was positive:

> In the exceptional circumstances of this application, I am prepared to treat February 1983 as the time from which compensation will be considered....

So everyone was greatly relieved and I could breathe again.

The joy was a little muted when I read in April the sad news that Lord Taylor had died. The obituaries were extremely complimentary. Apart from this charming man's incredibly successful legal career and the impact he made, I learnt that he was not only a Cambridge rugby blue, but also an accomplished musician into the bargain. Apart from his contribution to the justice system, he was also well regarded for his work chairing the public inquiry into the Hillsborough disaster and making wide-ranging recommendations for public safety whilst opposing the introduction of identity cards for football fans.

In this era of specialization, it is so gratifying to know that a man of such sound all-round talent can still reach the pinnacle of his profession and yet be so down-to-earth. *The Independent* reported an amusing story:

> Many who achieve high office acquire a self-importance to accompany it. It was not the case with Taylor. Once, when he said that he could not be pompous because he had three daughters, one had interrupted him to say that he could still be pompous but they could tell him when he was being so.

As a father of three vivacious and dynamic daughters myself, this was not entirely unfamiliar to me either. Thank heaven for little girls....

Now that I had received the green light to claim business loss, it was necessary to retain the services of a really top quality firm of accountants to prepare a detailed report and bring the assessment together.

Kormornick wisely suggested that we might employ one of the firms the Assessor had instructed in the past, Robson Rhodes, since they would be conversant with the assessment process and known to each other. I was hesitant at first. It seemed a little unconventional to use the government's expert as allegiance might have been an issue. But in the end, persuaded by Kormornick, I decided that there was nothing to fear from a close scrutiny of my case. Using Robson Rhodes made sound sense. It was a bold move indeed.

It was necessary to obtain prior approval of the Home Office. They willingly acceded to the request, though thought it a little odd that I had the temerity to use their own expert, who would examine my case most rigorously. So Kormornick introduced me to the canny, dry-witted Hugh Gregory, a partner from the Robson Rhodes' Bristol office specializing in forensic accounting. He was a very well respected expert with a huge amount of experience who had appeared as an expert witness in court many times.

A meeting was arranged in Bristol. As we travelled together in my antiquated grey Ford Sierra along the M4, Kormornick felt quite proud of the accounting brief he had prepared. This included a forty-six-page witness statement from me of more than 14,000 words, which had taken months to prepare and had quite exhausted us both.

I had a warm feeling about Gregory right from the start and the meeting went well. Gregory was assisted by Fred Brown, who was also very helpful. Kormornick had already provided them with a substantial amount of information and documents but the accountants required much more before Gregory was able to prepare his report.

He emphasized how much the Assessor was a stickler for detail, and so was he. But in fairness, Kormornick added, the Assessor was accountable to the Home Secretary, and neither was he able to hand out public funds without sufficient evidence. Thus, I would have to go back thirty years to provide a full history of the business from 1973 to 1983, ten years before the arrest, and the business plans for 1983 and after – a daunting task indeed.

In addition, I had to provide a very detailed employment history going back twenty-four years to the sale of Sterling in October 1983 in order to show that I had made reasonable efforts to find work and a decent income.

Though my first witness statement was extremely useful background material, Gregory now dictated an endless shopping list to Kormornick of the further information required. I could see him rolling his eyes to the heavens in horror contemplating the sheer volume of work yet to be undertaken.

I noticed that the list did not make any reference to the US losses.

"Hugh, what about the enormous losses caused because Customs prevented Sterling getting into the US market?"

"James, that can't be claimed because it wasn't established long enough. Sorry."

"But that seems so unfair … we were about to do so well there."

"You're right, but it's best to stick with what can be proved."

Kormornick reinforced this approach, which had underpinned all his successful cases working with Tonna. It had also worked extremely well in Reg's case. So, reluctantly, I accepted the advice, but with some disappointment. The US had represented an enormous opportunity for Sterling and I would end up receiving a fraction of my real losses.

It had been an exhausting meeting but we'd covered a huge amount of ground. Kormornick and I were overwhelmed by the sheer volume of detail and documents that would be required and our heads were spinning. For me, it was also a bitter reminder of everything lost over the last twenty-four years, the pain of having to dredge it all up yet again, and the endless questions and explanations. This was becoming just like the trial preparation ordeal once more, but much worse: this was a papers-only process and I had never before worked with such a thorough and demanding professional team.

As we travelled back to London along the M4, with the rain pounding the windscreen, our minds tried to focus on the Herculean task at hand and how to tackle it. Kormornick fired question after question at me. It was clear that we would have to spend many hours preparing the case and the supporting evidence, and that this could take many years. Even Kormornick, who was no slouch when it came to preparation, was amazed at the enormity of the task and the heavy burden on his client.

Over the next three months, we spent most weeks together preparing my next witness statement in order to provide the further detail required by Gregory. It was finished on 16 April and ran to a further ninety pages and 23,500 words. The two of us were exhausted again. But at least now, Gregory could prepare his report.

The weeks flew quickly by as Kormornick and I continued preparing the case as we awaited the accountancy report. It arrived in early June and ran to more than 100 pages. We spent many days checking through it to ensure that all the facts and figures were correct and nothing had been omitted. I even gave credit for the unpaid tax that had led to bankruptcy. It was an irony to think that the Inland Revenue would not lose out at all in the end.

The accounting report was then sent to the Home Office and the next step was to wait for a response. The Home Office had instructed Sally Longworth, of Grant Thornton. Longworth's report also landed on Kormornick's desk with a loud thud: it was more than 120 pages. It took us days to go over and raised a number of issues. Back we headed on the M4 towards Bristol for yet another exhausting meeting with Gregory.

It was another long and tiring day. The biggest issue that Longworth had raised was the future plans for Sterling after 1983. So after providing two witness statements totalling 153 pages and some 37,500 words, I was now required by the Assessor to provide yet another one with still more information.

The third witness statement amounted to ninety-five pages and 30,000 words. In all, we had provided the equivalent of a tome of 248 pages and 67,500 words. It's all a bit of a blur now. All I can remember is seemingly endless days and weeks spent with Kormornick and The Secretary drowning in hundreds of papers scattered everywhere and the endless questions and further questions and yet more action lists....

Longworth had also raised questions about my efforts to find suitable work after the sale of Sterling. Whilst I am sure that she felt she was only just doing her job and I didn't take it too personally, this suggestion was quite offensive and insensitive in the circumstances. My team were also quite surprised. We had provided so much detail of all my efforts to find work and the work I actually did, notwithstanding all the difficulties.

After the demands of the trial in 1985, I was literally on my knees having lost two businesses, and now my marriage was heading for the rocks. And employers were hardly queuing up for someone who'd just spent four weeks at the Bailey defending arms export charges.

So it was also necessary to obtain a detailed report from an employment expert, Keith Carter, running to more than thirty pages, dealing with my working history over twenty-two years and the numerous job applications I had made. This confirmed that I had made reasonable and best efforts to find and maintain employment after 1985.

Carter is a very genial and empathetic person. He couldn't believe what had happened to me. The meeting was positive and helpful, though it was tiring having to go through all the intimate detail with another person yet again, having to revisit all those memories that had been shut away and reflecting on what could have been....

It was an energy-sapping exercise, from which it took me a few days to recover. But in the end it was worth it because it seemed to answer all of Longworth's points, and Lord Brennan never questioned my attempts to mitigate my losses.

By far the worst experience was the interrogation into minute details of my personal life (the humiliation and degradation) and Kormornick's endless questioning – just sheer torture at times. This whole affair had damaged me and my family. I had tried to be as stoical as possible to put a brave face on things and just to get on with life as best as one can in the circumstances. And then there were some embarrassing questions about my marriage and divorce and intimate details about the effect on our relationship. It was really awful.

The absence of medical records was a real problem. Not being an introspective person by nature, and not believing in counselling or psychologists, there was no recorded history of my physical and psychological condition. I had not even visited the GP.

Marathon running and battling it out with the barristers in chambers and recalcitrant solicitors was the main form of rehab and it seemed to work rather well, though it was a little frustrating at times. And if that wasn't enough, there were always Sisi's cake stalls to cheer me up and keep me amused, though it is doubtful that the wet and windy days when I assisted in the cake selling, with incessant banal questions about icing and ingredients, did me much good. But May Waller was always there to help out. She has lasted well and ably assists in Sisi's frantic life. She could have dived for the exit on many occasions, but has displayed an unparalleled loyalty and has earned honorary full membership of the Edmiston family.

Kormornick explained to me that I would receive little or no credit for my efforts to minimize the effects on me. To the contrary; I could actually be worse off not having seen anyone to receive treatment and to record the history. This all seemed bizarre to me, but then the law does work in mysterious ways, as I had discovered only too well.

We wondered what way there was out of the dilemma and thought about whether it was worth my seeing a psychological expert so long after the event and considering some counselling. When Kormornick first mooted this, and that I could still be a basket case, I nearly punched him right on the nose. But I knew he meant well and it was just another one of his poor attempts at humour in order to persuade me that this may be in my best interest, because there were clearly some ongoing issues.

In the end, we decided that, in the circumstances, we would just provide the Assessor with full details about the personal effects without any expert report and leave it to his discretion. This was a most painful process having to revisit this in minute detail, and then the ordeal of having to read and re-read the draft witness statements and to confront the situation. Holding up the mirror to oneself, warts and all, is rarely a pleasant experience; the years had certainly taken their toll.

On many occasions, despite Kormornick's persistence, a few hours at a time was all that was barely tolerable, and often the day ended early by taking a late lunch and calling it quits. Lunch was always fun and Kormornick would try to humour me with his amusing little anecdotes and latest domestic crisis, as well as stories of the seemingly endless stream of new au pairs from all over the globe. The last one didn't stay too long after boarding a tube train leaving one of his daughters on the platform as the train departed. And if that wasn't enough, there were the stories of the neighbours. With a yappy Springer Spaniel for a secretary, he wasn't exactly the most popular person around....

At one stage, I was a bit concerned that Kormornick may have been losing his marbles too when he left The Secretary tied up against some railings in Oxford Street and only realized this some hours later. On his return, though, The Secretary was naturally delighted to be reunited with his master and greeted him with the usual affection. The two community officers standing ready were not greatly amused; they even threatened to take The Secretary into care were such a thing ever to happen again. In fairness though, he was entirely immersed in my case and so could be forgiven for the occasional absent-mindedness.

There has always been some drama in my life too, and the compensation case was to be no exception. While all the evidence was being collated and final submissions were being prepared, there was a most alarming turn of events. On 19 November 2007, Lord Brennan collapsed in the House of Lords shortly after concluding a speech on the Human Fertilization and Embryology Bill. Fortunately, there was doctor in the House, Baron Darzi, who gave heart massage, and Lord Brennan was admitted to St Thomas' Hospital, London, where he was fitted with a pacemaker and spent time recuperating.

Eventually, in December 2007, we were all in a position to prepare final submissions to the Assessor and these, together with several volumes of papers, were submitted to the Home Office in February 2008, twenty-five years after the arrests.

Kormornick and I were a trifle drained and could now do nothing more than wait a further six months for the assessment to be made, hoping that all would now proceed smoothly. But fate was to play its hand once more in December, when Lord Brennan again became unwell in the Chamber of the House of Lords. As he was thanking peers and staff who had been involved on the occasion when he was last taken ill, he fell back in his seat. Thankfully, he returned to good health and was in court in April 2008, leading the successful claim for the families of the victims of the Omagh bombing.

The six-month period had dragged by slowly as spring turned into summer and eventually the call came that the award would be ready for collection from Marsham Street that afternoon.

Wondering about the outcome, Kormornick and I had a carbo-loading Italian lunch at Zizzi in Wigmore Street and then made our way over to Westminster so that I could learn my appalling fate....

Chapter 30

Conclusion

"Well...?" exclaimed Lawrence Kormornick. Daydreaming, I was totally lost in thought. I looked up without uttering a word, and handed the letter over.

"Are you pleased?" Kormornick asked with pride swelling up in his chest, for justice had at last been done.

"I don't know, I just don't know," murmured I languidly.

"You should never have to worry again, and you can now live a comfortable life on the interest alone, if it stays at 6.5%, that is."

"I know. It's absolutely tremendous what you and the team have done for me, and I do appreciate it. And it shows that there is some justice after all in Merrie England, even if I've had to wait twenty-five years for it. And just think of those poor buggers unlucky enough to be deprived of any redress now that my scheme was abolished in 2006."

"You're welcome," Kormornick retorted. "Sad it's taken so long and thanks for being so patient. You were very lucky indeed to get in before the drawbridge went up."

"Nobody has ever given me this sort of money before," I mused.

"Yes, but you were wrongfully charged, and have never received an apology. The sum reflects only a relatively small part of what you've lost because of the actions of others. And how do you begin to compensate someone for the loss of twenty-five years? The truth is that it's impossible. And remember, James, you could have earned millions more from Sterling in the American market but, regrettably, it wasn't possible to include that in the claim."

"I know that," I replied. "It's just that I must now banish all doubt as to my own worth. I need to prove to myself that I'm still capable of success, irrespective of all the aggro, of being older and of having been compensated."

"Is that a good idea? You've taken a real beating over the last twenty-five years – you must be exhausted!"

"I know I may not be the man I was, but I have to find out how much I can still do."

"Well, how the devil are you going to do that and how can you really afford to take any risks now?" Kormornick knew that I had deteriorated mentally, but he was loathe to remind me of this.

"But I would like to try to do something."

"How?"

"I've thought long and hard. Manufacturing still appeals. I'll have to avoid the banks as I'm now too old in their eyes and that bankruptcy thing may still be hanging over me. Perhaps I'll make things again."

"But what are you going to make this time?"

"Well, sporting guns, I suppose, and I could always write another book…"

"What a great idea! You've got the knowledge and experience."

"But Lawrence, what about you?"

"Well, perhaps I'll just catch up with my family and The Secretary and then see. Still a lot to do on the bucket list. And I've always fancied becoming a mediator. Anyway, how about some skiing next year? We could certainly do with some fresh mountain air away from it all."

"Ok, you're on, so let's drink to that!"

I ran Kormornick back to Chiswick, passing through Notting Hill and Holland Park, and then wended our way along Chiswick High Road and down to the river. The pavement cafés in Chiswick were full of people relaxing outside enjoying the sunshine; now I could relax as well.

The reality was beginning to register, and we opted for a celebratory glass of claret at Café Rouge on Strand-on-the-Green near Kew Bridge. Just one, mind you, as I was driving.

It was a beautiful afternoon in all senses. We sat outside on the first floor watching the trees gently swaying and a swollen and glistening Father Thames roll by imperiously at high tide. This was a feeling I had not known for twenty-five years.

As our glasses clinked, I grinned. Kormornick smiled, not realizing the cause of my amusement. I always chuckle when visiting Café Rouge. I explained to him that my second daughter, Portia, now a respected City lawyer, when she was at university would take various vacation jobs to earn the spondulicks so sadly lacking from her impecunious father. She did everything, including tele-sales, at which she was highly successful and actually enjoyed. One such opportunity that arose was a local job at Café Rouge.

When she signed on at the local Café Rouge in Kensington, there was great excitement and expectation. Sadly, she struggled with the demands of waitressing and lasted only two days.

An exasperated manager put his arm around her shoulder sympathetically and earnestly informed her that she was, in fact, quite the worst waitress that he ever had the misfortune to employ. So there was no option; she had to go. Of course, she turned on the waterworks and blubbed out of hurt pride, but privately was the first to admit that he was absolutely correct. Luckily for the manager, at that time it was long before Portia had delved deep into the annals of employment law; not that that would have done her any good....

Life had suddenly taken a new course, so that one could now enjoy the lighter side of such memories and we laughed heartily about it and swopped many stories of similar disasters from student days.

While there, we took the opportunity of informing John Tonna and Hugh Gregory of what had just been revealed during our afternoon's discovery. There was excitement and congratulations all around and it had been a superb team effort. There was great delight at having achieved success for me and an enormous sense of relief.

Tonna and Gregory, though naturally delighted with the outcome for me, couldn't resist the temptation to extract details of the award from a legal and accounting perspective. This had been a complex case with diverse claims. The accounting experts had been battling it out with each other. I have to say that the legal and accounting submissions went right over my head so I left Kormornick to provide the nuts and bolts – the headlines were more than enough for me.

It was an extraordinary sensation to have the burden of the world lifted from my Atlas-like shoulders, while just enjoying the sun, the wine, and the river, without thought or need for anything further.

London was its very best; life was looking up for me; and now I could enjoy it all again.

Chapter 31

Edmiston Mk II

Today, I have a terraced house in Cornwall by the sea with a view of St Michael's Mount. It was totally rebuilt by Phil Eddy, the President of the Penzance Pirates Rugby Club, under Sally's competent supervision. I have also started a small gun-making company with a colleague, developing the guns in Britain, and the firm is about to start producing them in America with sub-contractors for the American market.

But my pride and joy is the production of traditional English side-by-side shotguns, one hundred per cent made in England, in which I have joined up with Peter Boxall, the former manufacturing director of Holland and Holland Ltd.

We both believe that the finest guns are still made in Britain. In order to be more competitive, the most modern and precise manufacturing methods must be employed so that the ultimate craftsmen's skills – so necessary to produce only the very best – are used to their greatest advantage. Kormornick is glad that I have not taken on this task on my own.

How much was the award that I received? Let's just say that it broke the all-time record and is unlikely to be beaten given that compensation for wrongful conviction has now been capped at a mere million pounds for those wrongfully imprisoned for ten years or more.

Rationale

This book has been written not as a saga of a twenty-five-year heroic struggle against the state where the odds were heavily stacked against me, but as a well-documented account of a miscarriage of justice that led to a personal tragedy, a family break-up, loss of a business and bankruptcy. This is something that most would hardly deem possible in England's green and pleasant land. Hopefully, no one else will ever have the misfortune to go through what I've suffered.

Although the best years of my adult life have been consumed in my battle for justice and restitution, I am now able to look back over the darkness of the past twenty-eight years and be thankful that I have been so lucky to have recovered any compensation at all. I have survived such an ordeal. My friend, Reg Dunk, was not as fortunate.

If it had not been for a whole series of fortuitous events that unfolded during the process of bringing this extraordinary affair to a conclusion, I would never have recovered compensation and cleared my name, and would probably have ended my life in dire straits. These included:

- my acquittal through the dedicated efforts of my lawyers, David Barnard, Robin Auld and John Manuell
- the acquittal of the Matrix Churchill directors after Mr Justice Smedley's bold decision to uphold the submission of Geoffrey Robertson QC to order disclosure of secret documents that led to the Scott Inquiry
- John Major setting up the Scott Inquiry and giving him enormous scope in the terms of reference for such a thorough investigation and report that led to the quashing of Dunk's conviction
- Lord Justice Scott's unearthing of evidence that proved Dunk's embassy witnesses had been blocked and the fierce questioning of Stephen Egerton by him and Presiley Baxendale QC that led to the quashing of Dunk's conviction

- The submissions of Godfrey Carey QC at Dunk's appeal
- The quashing of Dunk's conviction by Lord Chief Justice Taylor, Lord Justice Ognall and Lord Justice Gage, opening the way to compensation for him and for me
- The submissions of Edward Fitzgerald QC and Nicholas Bowen QC, which established the meaning of the ex gratia scheme that paved the way for Redemption
- Mr Justice Henriques' quashing of the Home Secretary's decision on the custody requirement, thus clearing the way for me
- the Home Secretary, Charles Clarke, for admitting the Matrix Churchill Directors and me to the discretionary scheme
- Lawrence Kormornick finding a loophole in the opaque government scheme shortly before its sudden and unexpected withdrawal, and for guiding me through the rigorous and serpentine assessment process
- Payne Hicks Beach keeping my papers going back twenty-four years
- John Tonna's compelling eighty-page submissions
- Hugh Gregory's formidable accounting report
- Keith Carter's cogent employment report
- Lord Brennan QC's making of such a fair assessment
- And the loyal support of my nineteen witnesses: Stephen Adamson: Jeffrey Bonas; David Bryans; Sir Tim Chessells; Tony Durrant; Sisi Edmiston; Scarlett Edmiston; Steve James; Sally Laird; Judge John Manuell; James Mayne; Fred Meier Jr; John Olsen; Roma Skinner; Michael Slade; Anthony Slingsby; David Stride; Peter Swain; and Roy Swainbank.

I give thanks to all these people.

I also give thanks to my mother, Lady Drumalbyn; Pandora Edmiston; Portia Edmiston; Harry Edmiston; the late Reg Dunk; the late Major Keen; David Howroyd; Keith Cole; Guy Green; Fred Brown and all the team at Robson Rhodes; Maurice Robson; the loyal workforce at Sterling who helped me to make a dream come true; the

Kormornick family for welcoming me into their home and letting me steal Lawrence away for three years; and, last but not least, "The Secretary".

My eternal gratitude to our editors, Linne Matthews and Paul Rosenberg, an Oxford contemporary who was unlucky in his bid to become the university's Professor of Poetry. As an English specialist, he has cast a correcting eye over the script. The resultant amendments in basic English usage were legion, to the extent that a further three months were added to the book's preparation. Any further obvious howlers can be placed firmly at the door of Rosie's American citizenship.

This has been a sorry tale indeed but it is still to this country's eternal credit that these wrongs were exposed and eventually remedied. Hopefully, there will be fewer miscarriages of justice in the future so that no one else has to go through all this.

The individual perpetrators who were responsible for such conduct/errors and/or omissions apparently have never been brought to book. Rather, they have retired on index-linked pensions with attractively enameled national awards to be worn only on occasions where the dictates of the dress code specify white tie and tails.

An internet search has revealed that Patrick Nixon retired from FCO in 2004 after serving two years as High Commissioner in Zambia and then becoming our man in Abu Dhabi. After his appointment as Director of FCO Services in 2006, Carsten Pigott left in 2010 to become a founder member and consultant of Intercultural Management (ICM). ICM offers training and workshops to help prepare executives and diplomats for international assignments.

Not only have the "machinations" of Customs & Excise and the Foreign & Commonwealth Office been exposed, but so also have government lunacy in procurement in the arcane field of small arms, not only in the context of Sterling, but also in a minor way, with BSA.

The irony is that had the government not prosecuted the Matrix Churchill directors or abandoned the case at an early stage, they could have avoided the Scott Inquiry and all that ensued, and in particular, the revelations in my case. Some would contend that it was a misjudgment of massive proportions but I couldn't possibly comment.... I wonder who had ultimate control of the final decision and where he/she is today? Probably on some desert island on that government gold-plated, index-linked pension. Presumably such a thing is unlikely to ever happen again given that Customs has been merged with the Inland Revenue, and they are now collectively known as HM Revenue and Customs.

Mention must also be made of the sheer world quality that firms like Sterling and Matrix Churchill Ltd produced in their respective fields of manufacturing expertise due to the dedication of their loyal employees, who have gone uncompensated. Quite apart from the high overhead costs that successive governments have inflicted on such manufacturing entities in Britain, these firms were employers of substantial numbers of long-standing and skilled personnel with a huge pride and loyalty to those companies. The irresponsibility of dashing the reputations of these concerns lies firmly with government and is madness personified.

Another not unconnected scandal resulting from all this is one of cost and the tremendous waste, which is a matter of some relevance today. All the Arms-to-Iraq prosecutions ended in acquittal or were quashed on appeal. The costs of mounting the prosecutions, court costs, legal aid costs, the cost of compensation and assessment, and the cost of the Scott Inquiry, are thought to have conservatively exceeded £50 million. Since the poor taxpayer is funding this, that oft-used cliché "the public has a right to know" has never been truer, and it is also germane to all this. How many schools and hospitals could have been built instead?

I've also mentioned the complete fiasco of small arms procurement, and in particular, the SA-80 service rifle, which was adopted at huge initial cost. The fact that the German firm of Messrs Heckler & Koch GmbH won a closed contract for more than 60,000,000 Euros to make those rifles function properly, is nothing short of scandalous. And the further point of originally providing our armed forces with sub-standard equipment is nothing short of criminal.

It is for all these reasons that this book has been written. But there remains one further important reason. Though the Home Office has accepted that there was a serious default by a public authority, the one clear factor lacking has been a single word – "SORRY".

The miscarriage of justice that resulted in a living hell for me has never resulted in an apology from any quarter. The late Reg Dunk never received a public apology either, and, sadly, compensation arrived too late for him to benefit. Has anyone caught up in the Arms-to-Iraq scandal ever received a public apology, and if not, why not?

The withdrawal of the Home Secretary's ex gratia scheme in April 2006 also means that many victims of miscarriage of justice will now go uncompensated.

Given this lack of accountability, it defies belief that the former Commissioner of the Metropolitan Police, Sir Paul Stephenson, had been lobbying the Home Secretary to make it even more difficult for people to obtain redress from the police for wrongful actions! This smacked of the attempt by the officials in my case to avoid any responsibility by relying on immunity from suit.

Critics say that the police are trying to put themselves above the rule of law and to undermine constitutional safeguards against abuses of power, already weak enough, especially after the abolition of the ex gratia compensation scheme in 2006. As one solicitor, Louise Christian, has commented:

> It's clearly an attempt by the police to escape the rule of law. When access to justice is denied, the principle of the rule of law is damaged. The rich and powerful can always go to court; it's people without means who can't.

Perhaps the best reason for being harsh with Whitehall is echoed in the words of Judge Holt, who had fined the overenthusiastic coppers for blocking voters' rights in 1703:

If public officers willingly infringe men's rights they ought to pay greater damages.... The punishment will make public officers more careful to observe the constitution.

Three hundred years on, an indulgent Whitehall gives its public officers precious few deterrents not to "infringe men's rights", and extremely limited redress for victims.

James Edmiston
June 2012

End Note

Looking back now over twenty-five years, there is a great sense of pride and satisfaction in having been able to persuade the Home Secretary to put right this miscarriage of justice. Law is a demanding profession, physically, mentally and emotionally. There can be many long hours, low points, disappointments and frustrations. But every so often it is so rewarding to be part of something extraordinary and to make a difference. Many people played a part in the Redemption and I thank them for making it possible.

On a personal level, a man's reputation, dignity and financial security have been restored and James is now able to tell this incredible story. On a professional level, it is reassuring to know that a miscarriage of justice was put right and the system eventually worked well. However, the future is uncertain; others may be less fortunate because the ex gratia scheme was withdrawn in 2006. Perhaps if the Justice Minister, Ken Clarke, were to read *The Sterling Redemption*, he may be inclined to re-introduce a suitable scheme to compensate the victims of a miscarriage of justice who have been wrongly charged, to operate in conjunction with the wrongful conviction scheme. Something would be better than nothing; even if absent of compensation, the government could at least say "sorry" to the victims and their families.

The Sterling Redemption still poses many unanswered questions. Although the book does allow a rare glimpse into the inner workings of government departments, we may still never uncover the full story of why James was prosecuted. Lord Justice Scott was unable to go back any earlier than 1984 to unearth how high decisions actually went and, in particular, who knew about the "friendly words" with the embassies.

It is astonishing to think how the government could have allowed James' prosecution and, more importantly, the Matrix Churchill prosecution to go ahead. They tried to explain to Customs continually that they had got it completely wrong but they stubbornly refused to listen and were determined to proceed with the prosecutions regardless of the consequences. Surely, someone in government must have realized the significance and should have intervened to drop the charges? The sensational revelations and criticism of the Scott Inquiry and the massive damage inflicted on Whitehall could have been so easily avoided had the Matrix Churchill case not been prosecuted or had it been discontinued before trial. Historians will, no doubt, long debate the question in order to find some answers.

In the end, the reader is left to draw their own conclusions about the investigation and prosecution, and whether this could ever happen again. Readers may also wish to speculate on the inner workings of government departments with their own separate agendas, and why innocent people have had to suffer unnecessarily to avoid government embarrassment. In *The Justice Game* (1998) Geoffrey Robertson QC gives an enlightening view of how the state operates:

> When under threat, the state protects itself instinctively, like an octopus disturbed by a stick. The coils swirl in different directions, the overall pattern is unplanned, but the motive is always self-protection: damage to others is incidental.

His verdict on the Scott Report perhaps offers a clue as to what happened in James' case:

> Scott exculpated the makers of these decisions because they sincerely believed it was for the best. But their sincerity stemmed from the improper assumption that protection of the state is more important than justice to the individual or honesty to Parliament.

The Scott Inquiry was unique and a political landmark. According to Richard Norton-Taylor, the author of *Truth is a Difficult Concept: Inside the Scott Inquiry* (1995):

> Government lawyers conspired with civil servants to suppress embarrassing and damaging information. When they were found out, civil servants blamed each other, or ministers, while ministers blamed their officials in what became the biggest buck-passing operation in the history of Whitehall.... Whitehall will do its utmost to ensure that never again will a judge be given such freedom to conduct a public inquiry into the activities of government.

It has been a privilege to work with James and an excellent professional team on the case as well as on this book. After his acquittal in 1985, by necessity, many emotions had been locked away to enable him to get on with his life in order to survive. The case meant his having endlessly to rake over the events of a twenty-five-year period and to confront many unpleasant memories and consequences for him and his family.

He had to work tirelessly on providing reams of information and share with me, his professional team and the Independent Assessor, a great deal of intimate detail, and I am sorry for having had to put him and his family through such an ordeal. To look back at what could have been must have been a painful process, to say the least. Throughout all this, he never lost his dignity and sense of humour, and we have become good friends. If some good has come of the case and this book, then surely it will have been worth all of the time and effort.

No justice system is infallible. On an optimistic note, one gives thanks (and it is a source of great pride) that we still live in a country with, arguably, the best justice system in the world where good men will not hesitate to put a miscarriage right.

Many played a part in the Redemption and are rightly acknowledged by James. In particular, Lord Chief Justice Taylor and Lord Justice Scott had little hesitation in denouncing the behaviour of the officials; Mr Justice Henriques gave a robust interpretation of the ex gratia scheme; and the Home Secretary, Charles Clarke, admitted James into the scheme. This allowed the Independent

Assessor, Lord Brennan QC, to make a fair and reasonable award and to find that, "The circumstances of this application reveal a miscarriage of justice that has led to a personal tragedy, a broken family and the loss of a business...."

Hopefully, there will be fewer miscarriages of justice in the future, and any will be put right swiftly, and perhaps one day, someone in government and the officials who blocked the witnesses might actually say "sorry" to James and his family; that would certainly mean a lot to them.

Lawrence Kormornick
June 2012

Also by James Edmiston, *The Sterling Years: Small Arms and the Men*, first published in 1992.

This is an account of selling and marketing Sterling equipment worldwide and the downfall of his company in 1985.

The products were sold in around a hundred countries and the "battleship" engineering of the Mark 4 sub-machine gun won the product the reputation of being the world's most reliable automatic weapon of all time.

Sterling was engaged almost entirely in export, and there is probably no other (British) defence company that can boast a similar record of success.

The demise of Sterling came about through conduct by authority that most Britons would not deem possible in a Western democracy.